First Edition

Common Core
Support Coach

TARGET Foundational Mathematics 8

Dr. Jerry Kaplan
Senior Mathematics Consultant

Common Core Support Coach, Target: Foundational Mathematics, First Edition, Grade 8
T203NA   ISBN-13: 978-1-61997-979-6
Contributing Writers: TSI Graphics   **Cover Design:** Q2A/Bill Smith

Triumph Learning® 136 Madison Avenue, 7th Floor, New York, NY 10016

Contents

1 Irrational Numbers

PLUG IN Understanding Rational Numbers

A **rational number** can be written as a ratio of two integers.

Examples of rational numbers:

$$5 \text{ or } \frac{5}{1}, \frac{2}{3}, \frac{-5}{8},$$

$$1\frac{1}{12} \text{ or } \frac{13}{12}, -9 \text{ or } \frac{-9}{1}$$

Every rational number can be written as a decimal form that either terminates or repeats.

A **terminating decimal** can be written with a limited number of decimal places without changing its value.

Examples:

$$12 = 12.0 = 12.00 = 12.000$$
$$4\frac{1}{10} = 4.1 = 4.10 = 4.100$$
$$-6 = -6.0 = -6.00 = -6.000$$
$$\frac{-9}{10} = -0.9 = -0.90 = -0.900$$

A **repeating decimal** cannot be written with a limited number of decimal places without changing its value. Repeating decimals have a digit or a series of digits that repeat.

Examples:

$3.\overline{6}$ means 6 repeats forever.

$-2.\overline{53}$ means 53 repeats forever.

$0.1\overline{7}$ means 7 repeats forever.

I see that an integer or mixed number is a rational number because both can be written as a ratio with two integers, too.

I see! I can write any number of 0s to the right of the last decimal place without changing its value.

I get it! I can write a repeating decimal by placing a bar over the digit or digits that repeat.

Words to Know

rational number
a number that can be written as the ratio of two integers

terminating decimal
a decimal that has a limited number of decimal places

repeating decimal
a decimal that has a digit that repeats or a series of digits that repeat

DISCUSS What is the difference between 0.24 and 0.$\overline{24}$? Which is greater? How do you know?

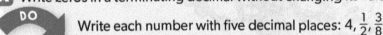

A Write zeros in a terminating decimal without changing its value.

DO Write each number with five decimal places: $4, \frac{1}{2}, \frac{3}{8}$

➊ Write each number as a decimal.

$4 = $ _____ $\frac{1}{2} = $ _____ $\frac{3}{8} = $ _____

➋ Write zeros to the right of the last decimal place to end up with five decimal places.

4._____   0.5_____   0.375_____

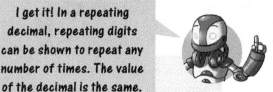

I get it! In a repeating decimal, repeating digits can be shown to repeat any number of times. The value of the decimal is the same.

B You can express a repeating decimal in different ways.

DO   Represent each as a repeating decimal to six decimal places: $-1.\overline{712}$, $\frac{2}{3}$, $0.\overline{68}$.

1 Write each number as a decimal.

$-1.\overline{712} =$ _____ $\frac{2}{3} =$ _____ $0.\overline{68} =$ _____

2 Continue the repeating digits to the sixth decimal place. Put a bar over the last repeating digit(s).

$-1.\overline{712} =$ _____

$0.\overline{6} =$ _____

$0.\overline{68} =$ _____

C You can write some rational numbers equivalently with fewer digits.

DO   Write each rational number with the fewest digits possible: $6.2222\overline{2}$, -0.10300, $1.135\overline{35}$, $0.736888\overline{8}$, 7.500, 0.00010.

1 Identify each number as a repeating or terminating decimal.

Terminating: _____, _____, _____

Repeating: _____, _____,

_____

2 Rewrite the repeating decimals so that the digit or digits that repeat appear only once below a bar.

$6.2222\overline{2} =$ _____

$1.135\overline{35} =$ _____

3 Rewrite the terminating decimals so the last non-zero digit to the right is the final digit.

$0.736888\overline{8} =$ _____

$-0.10300 =$ _____

$7.500 =$ _____

$0.00010 =$ _____

DISCUSS   Tevin says $0.15\overline{15}$ is the same as $0.\overline{15}$. Do you agree? Explain.

PRACTICE

Write the numbers with 8 digits to the right of the decimal point.

1 14 _____

2 2.793 _____

3 $0.\overline{57}$ _____

4 $1.74\overline{596}$ _____

Write the numbers with as few digits as possible.

5 722.000000000 _____

6 $1.55555555\overline{5}$ _____

7 $3.385385385\overline{385}$ _____

8 $0.41276276276\overline{276}$ _____

Some numbers have decimal expansions that neither repeat nor terminate. They are called **irrational numbers**.

6.931558...

0.4198174...

> I see! The three dots mean the number continues forever, but there is no pattern in the order of the digits shown.

π is one example of an irrational number.

$$\pi = 3.14159...$$

Some **square roots** are irrational numbers.

$$\sqrt{3} = 1.732...$$

> I remember! π is used in the circumference and area formulas for circles: $C = \pi d$ and $A = \pi r^2$.

Together, rational and irrational numbers form the set of **real numbers**.

$$\frac{4}{9} = 0.\overline{4}$$
$$\sqrt{10} = 3.162...$$
$$-7 = -7.0$$

> I get it! Positive and negative numbers can be rational or irrational, and 0 is rational.

Words to Know

irrational number
a number whose decimal form does not repeat or terminate

48.395620475...

square root
one of two equal factors of a number whose square is equal to that number

$4 \times 4 = 16$, so 4 is the square root of 16.

$\sqrt{5} \times \sqrt{5} = 5$, so $\sqrt{5}$ is the square root of 5

real number
a rational number or an irrational number

7.28

53.535982...

$0.\overline{3}$

0

DISCUSS Are there any real numbers that are neither rational nor irrational? Are there any real numbers that are both rational and irrational?

A You can classify real numbers by their decimal form.

DO State whether the numbers are rational or irrational: 7, $-\frac{2}{9}$, $0.12627...$, $1\frac{1}{4}$

① Write each fraction or mixed number as a decimal.

$-\frac{2}{9} =$ _____, $1\frac{1}{4} =$ _____

② Determine whether the number has a decimal form that terminates, repeats, or does neither.

Terminating	Repeating	Neither
_____	_____	_____

7 is _____. $-\frac{2}{9}$ is _____.

0.12627... is _____. $1\frac{1}{4}$ is _____.

③ State whether each number is rational or irrational.

B You can classify real numbers by their decimal form.

> A perfect square is any integer times itself. So the square root of a perfect square is rational.

DO

State whether the numbers are rational or irrational: $\sqrt{21}$, $\sqrt{4}$, $\sqrt{\pi}$, $\sqrt{15}$, $\sqrt{36}$, $\sqrt{1}$. Write rational numbers in simplest form.

1 Determine if each number is square root of a perfect square.

2 State whether each number is rational or irrational.

3 Write each rational number in simplest form.

Square root of a perfect square: _____,
_____, _____

Not the square root of a perfect square: _____,
_____, _____

Rational: _____, _____, _____

Irrational: _____, _____, _____

$\sqrt{4} =$ _____

$\sqrt{36} =$ _____

$\sqrt{1} =$ _____

DISCUSS

Joe learns that people sometimes use $\frac{22}{7}$ for π. He writes $\pi = \frac{22}{7}$. Use what you know about rational and irrational numbers to explain why Joe is incorrect.

PRACTICE

**State whether each number is rational or irrational.
Write each rational number as a decimal in simplest form.**

1 $17.34\overline{05}$

_____

2 $\frac{3}{4}$

_____

3 $58.539035\ldots$

_____

4 $\sqrt{25}$

_____

5 $\sqrt{5}\ldots$

_____

6 π

_____

7 $\sqrt{51}\ldots$

_____

8 $3\frac{1}{6}$

_____

Use a rational approximation to the nearest hundredth to plot $\sqrt{5}$ on the number line.

1 Approximate $\sqrt{5}$ to the nearest integer. Since 5 is between 4 and 9, $\sqrt{5}$ is between 2 and 3. Because 5 is closer to 4 than to 9, $\sqrt{5}$ is closer to 2.

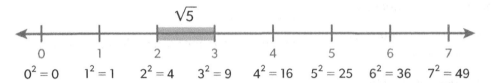

$$0^2 = 0 \quad 1^2 = 1 \quad 2^2 = 4 \quad 3^2 = 9 \quad 4^2 = 16 \quad 5^2 = 25 \quad 6^2 = 36 \quad 7^2 = 49$$

2 Approximate $\sqrt{5}$ to the nearest tenth.
Since 5 is between 4.84 and 5.29, $\sqrt{5}$ is between 2.2 and 2.3.
Because 5 is closer to 4.84 than to 5.29, $\sqrt{5}$ is closer to 2.2.

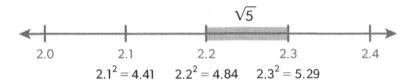

$$2.1^2 = 4.41 \quad 2.2^2 = 4.84 \quad 2.3^2 = 5.29$$

3 Approximate $\sqrt{5}$ to the nearest hundredth.
Since 5 is between 4.9729 and 5.0176, $\sqrt{5}$ is between 2.23 and 2.24.
Because 5 is closer to 5.0176 than to 4.9729, $\sqrt{5}$ is closer to 2.24.

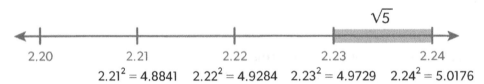

$$2.21^2 = 4.8841 \quad 2.22^2 = 4.9284 \quad 2.23^2 = 4.9729 \quad 2.24^2 = 5.0176$$

$\sqrt{5} \approx 2.24$ to the nearest hundredth.

 Why does the location of an irrational number on a number line need to be approximated?

LESSON LINK

PLUG IN	POWER UP	GO!
Rational numbers can be expressed as decimals that terminate or repeat.	Irrational numbers cannot be expressed as decimals that repeat or terminate.	*I see! I can approximate irrational numbers using rational numbers.*

WORK TOGETHER

Approximate $\sqrt{11}$ to the nearest hundredth without a number line.

- Find the integers whose squares are just above and just below 11.

- Find the tenths whose squares are just above and just below 11.

- Find the hundredths whose squares are just above and just below 11.

To the nearest hundredth, $\sqrt{11} \approx 3.32$.

$3^2 = 9$ and $4^2 = 16$
11 is closer to 9 than to 16, so $\sqrt{11}$ is closer to 3 than to 4.

$3.3^2 = 10.89$ and $3.4^2 = 11.56$
11 is closer to 10.89 than to 11.56, so $\sqrt{11}$ is closer to 3.3 than to 3.4.

$3.31^2 = 10.9561$ and $3.32^2 = 11.0224$
11 is closer to 11.0224 than to 10.9561, so $\sqrt{11}$ is closer to 3.32 than to 3.31.

A You can use squares to approximate decimal places of a square root.

DO Approximate $\sqrt{8}$ to the nearest hundredth.

1. Find the integers whose squares are on either side of 8.

2. Find the tenths whose squares are on either side of 8.

3. Find the hundredths whose squares are on either side of 8.

$2^2 = $ _____ and $3^2 = $ _____

8 is closer to _____ than to _____,

so $\sqrt{8}$ is close to _____.

$2.8^2 = $ _____ and $2.9^2 = $ _____

8 is closer to _____, so $\sqrt{8}$ is close to _____.

$2.82^2 = $ _____ and $2.83^2 = $ _____

8 is closer to _____, so $\sqrt{8}$ is close to _____.

To the nearest hundredth, $\sqrt{8} \approx$ _____.

B You can use approximations to compare irrational numbers.

DO Which is greater, $5\sqrt{11}$ or $6\sqrt{8}$? Use the previous calculations.

1. Find the approximation of the irrational factor.

2. Multiply each approximation by the rational factors.

3. Compare the approximations.

$\sqrt{11} \approx 3.32$ $\sqrt{8} \approx$ _____

$5\sqrt{11} \approx$ _____ × _____ = _____

$6\sqrt{8} \approx$ _____ × _____ = _____

_____ is greater than _____,

so _____ is greater than _____.

DISCUSS How can Greg use the following true statement to compare irrational numbers greater than 1? "If x and y are each greater than 1 and the square of x is greater than the square of y, then x is greater than y."

PRACTICE

Approximate each irrational number to the nearest hundredth.

1 $\sqrt{2}$

____

2 $\sqrt{6}$

> **REMEMBER**
> Approximate to the nearest integer, then to the nearest tenth, and then to the nearest hundredth.

____

3 $\sqrt{12}$

____

4 $\sqrt{20}$

> **HINT**
> You can check your answer by multiplying it by itself.

____

Approximate the following to the nearest hundredth. Use your answers to problem 1 and $\pi \approx 3.14$ to approximate each irrational factor.

5 $2\sqrt{2}$

_____

6 3π

_____

7 $\frac{\pi}{2}$

_____

8 $\pi\sqrt{2}$

_____

Approximate each product to the nearest thousandth. Then state which value is greater.

9 $3\sqrt{7}$ and $5\sqrt{2}$

_____ is

greater than _____.

$3\sqrt{7} \approx$ _____

$5\sqrt{2} \approx$ _____

10 $5\sqrt{6}$ and $6\sqrt{5}$

_____ is

greater than _____.

$5\sqrt{6} \approx$ _____

$6\sqrt{5} \approx$ _____

I remember! I multiply the approximation of the irrational factor by the rational factor to approximate their product.

DISCUSS

See the Pattern.

Adrian says he knows which of the two values below is greater without doing any calculations. What is Adrian's strategy?

$9\sqrt{11}$ and $9\sqrt{10}$

PROBLEM SOLVING

PAINTING A CIRCLE

READ

Max needs to bring wooden boards to a construction site. His truck can hold a board that is up to 8 ft long. Will his truck hold a board that is $2\sqrt{15}$ ft long? Find the length of the board to the nearest thousandth.

PLAN

• What are you asked to find? _____

• What do you need to know? _____

• How do you solve the problem? _____

SOLVE

❶ Find the integers whose squares are just above and just below 15.

_____^{2} = 9 and _____^{2} = 16

$\sqrt{15}$ is closer to _____.

❷ Find the tenths whose squares are just above and just below 15.

$3.8^2 =$ _____, $3.9^2 =$ _____

$\sqrt{15}$ is closer to _____.

❸ Find the hundredths whose squares are just above and just below 15.

$3.87^2 =$ _____, $3.88^2 =$ _____

$\sqrt{15}$ is closer to _____.

❹ Find the thousandths whose squares are just above and just below 15.

$3.872^2 =$ _____,

$3.873^2 =$ _____

$\sqrt{15}$ is closer to _____.

❺ Find the product of the rational approximation and 2.

$2 \times$ _____ = _____ ft

CHECK

Divide the product by 2. Then square the quotient. The solution should be very close to 15.

_____ $\div 2 =$ _____

_____ $^2 =$ _____

So, $2\sqrt{15} =$ _____.

> I can work backward to check my answer. That can show me if I've made a mistake in my calculations.

The length of the board to the nearest thousandth is _____ ft.

The board _____ inside the bed of the Max's truck.

PRACTICE

Use the problem-solving steps to help you.

1 Two legs of a right triangle measure 4 cm and 7 cm. The length of its hypotenuse is $\sqrt{65}$. Approximate the length of the hypotenuse to the nearest thousandth.

CHECKLIST
- [ ] READ
- [ ] PLAN
- [ ] SOLVE
- [ ] CHECK

2 The area of the square floor measures 107 ft². Find the approximate length of each side of the floor by approximating $\sqrt{107}$ to the nearest thousandth.

CHECKLIST
- [ ] READ
- [ ] PLAN
- [ ] SOLVE
- [ ] CHECK

3 Gary wants to rent space at the community garden. He can choose one space with an area of $16\sqrt{17}$ ft² and another space with an area of $17\sqrt{15}$ ft². If Gary wants to rent the larger plot, which should he choose? Explain.

CHECKLIST
- [ ] READ
- [ ] PLAN
- [ ] SOLVE
- [ ] CHECK

Square Roots and Cube Roots

PLUG IN Evaluating Square Numbers

You can write repeated multiplication as a **power**. The **base** is the repeated factor. The **exponent** is the number of times the factor repeats.

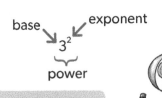

base → 3^2 ← exponent

power

To evaluate a base raised to an exponent, write a multiplication expression with the base for each factor. The exponent indicates the number of times the base is used as a factor.

$$7^2 = 7 \times 7 = 49$$

When you evaluate an integer base with an exponent of 2, the resulting integer is called a **square number**.

You read 4^2 as "4 squared."

Since $4^2 = 16$,

16 is a square number.

I see! The exponent is written above and to the right of the base.

I get it! The base is the number you multiply, and the exponent tells you how many factors there are.

So any integer that can be written as a power with an exponent of 2 is a square number.

Words to Know

power	**base**	**exponent**	**square number**
an expression of repeated multiplication	the repeated factor in a power	the raised number in a power that indicates the number of times the base is used as a factor	the product of an integer multiplied by itself
5^2 is the second power of 5.	base ↗ 5^2	5^2 ↖ exponent	Since $5^2 = 25$, 25 is a square number.
5^3 is the third power of 5.			

DISCUSS

Paulo says that 8^2 equals 16 because $8 \times 2 = 16$. How would you help Paulo correct his mistake?

A You can multiply to evaluate square numbers.

DO Evaluate 6^2, 8^2, and 1^2.

① Write the power as repeated multiplication

$6^2 = 6 \times$ ____, $8^2 =$ ____ $\times$ ____, $1^2 =$ ____ $\times$ ____

$6 \times 6 =$ ____, $8 \times 8 =$ ____, $1 \times 1 =$ ____

② Multiply.

B You can write repeated multiplication of two identical factors as a power.

DO Write 5×5 and 2×2 as powers.

❶ Identify the base.

❷ Identify the exponent.

❸ Write the power.

5×5

The base is _____.

The exponent is _____.

$5 \times 5 = \boxed{}^{\boxed{}}$

2×2

The base is _____.

The exponent is _____.

$2 \times 2 = \boxed{}^{\boxed{}}$

C You can evaluate expressions that include powers.

DO Evaluate $7^2 - 2^2$.

❶ Evaluate each power in the expression.

❷ Carry out the remaining operations.

$7^2 - 2^2$

$= 7 \times \rule{1.5cm}{0.4pt} - \rule{1.5cm}{0.4pt} \times \rule{1.5cm}{0.4pt}$

$= 49 - \rule{1.5cm}{0.4pt}$

$\rule{1.5cm}{0.4pt} - \rule{1.5cm}{0.4pt} = \rule{1.5cm}{0.4pt}$

> I remember! The order of operations says that I have to multiply before I add or subtract.

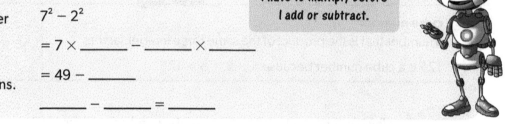

DISCUSS Simon and Ada evaluate $4^2 + 5^2$ differently. Simon says to add first, and then evaluate 9^2. Ada says to evaluate 4^2 and 5^2 first, and then add. Who is right, and why?

PRACTICE

Evaluate each power.

❶ 10^2

$\rule{1.5cm}{0.4pt} \times \rule{1.5cm}{0.4pt} = \rule{1.5cm}{0.4pt}$

❷ 15^2

$\rule{1.5cm}{0.4pt} \times \rule{1.5cm}{0.4pt} = \rule{1.5cm}{0.4pt}$

Write each repeated multiplication as a power.

❸ 7×7

$\rule{1.5cm}{0.4pt}$

❹ 12×12

$\rule{1.5cm}{0.4pt}$

Evaluate each expression.

❺ $5^2 + 10^2$

$= \rule{1.5cm}{0.4pt} \times \rule{1.5cm}{0.4pt} + \rule{1.5cm}{0.4pt} \times \rule{1.5cm}{0.4pt}$

$= \rule{1.5cm}{0.4pt} + \rule{1.5cm}{0.4pt}$

$= \rule{1.5cm}{0.4pt}$

❻ $9^2 - 3^2$

$= \rule{1.5cm}{0.4pt} \times \rule{1.5cm}{0.4pt} - \rule{1.5cm}{0.4pt} \times \rule{1.5cm}{0.4pt}$

$= \rule{1.5cm}{0.4pt} - \rule{1.5cm}{0.4pt}$

$= \rule{1.5cm}{0.4pt}$

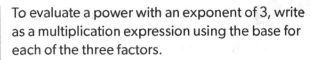

POWER UP — Evaluating Cube Numbers

When you raise an integer to the 3rd power, the result is called a **cube number**.

2^3 is read as "2 cubed."

To evaluate a power with an exponent of 3, write as a multiplication expression using the base for each of the three factors.

$$4^3 = 4 \times 4 \times 4 = 16 \times 4 = 64$$

> I get it! Any power with an exponent of 3 is equal to a cube number.

> I see! 64 is a cube number because it is equal to 4^3.

Words to Know

cube number
a number that is the product of the same three integer factors

125 is a cube number because $5 \times 5 \times 5 = 125$.

DISCUSS Why is a cube a good model for a cube number, such as 125?

A You can multiply to evaluate cube numbers.

DO Evaluate 10^3 and 3^3.

1. Write the power as repeated multiplication.

$10^3 = $ _____ $\times$ _____ $\times$ _____, $3^3 = $ _____ $\times$ _____ $\times$ _____

$10 \times 10 \times 10 = $ _____, $3 \times 3 \times 3 = $ _____

2. Multiply.

B You can write repeated multiplication of three identical factors as a power.

> I remember! The number being multiplied is the base. The number of times the base is used as a factor is the exponent.

DO Write $8 \times 8 \times 8$ and $2 \times 2 \times 2$ as powers.

1. Identify the base.

$8 \times 8 \times 8$ $\qquad$ $2 \times 2 \times 2$

2. Identify the exponent.

The base is _____. $\qquad$ The base is _____.

The exponent is _____. $\qquad$ The exponent is _____.

3. Write the power.

$8 \times 8 \times 8 = \square^{\square}$ $\qquad$ $2 \times 2 \times 2 = \square^{\square}$

To find a cube number, I can multiply the first two factors, then multiply that product by the third factor. So 2 × 2 × 2 is 4 × 2, or 8.

C You can evaluate expressions with cube numbers.

DO Evaluate $2^3 + 4^3$.

① Evaluate each power in the expression.

$$2^3 + 4^3$$

$$= 2 \times \underline{\hspace{1cm}} \times \underline{\hspace{1cm}} + \underline{\hspace{1cm}} \times \underline{\hspace{1cm}} \times \underline{\hspace{1cm}}$$

② Carry out the remaining operations.

$$= 8 + \underline{\hspace{1cm}}$$

$$= \underline{\hspace{1cm}}$$

DISCUSS Hector says that 1 is a square number. Maggie says that 1 is a cube number. Who is correct? Explain.

PRACTICE

Evaluate each power.

1 9^3

$$= \underline{\hspace{1cm}} \times \underline{\hspace{1cm}} \times \underline{\hspace{1cm}}$$

$$= \underline{\hspace{1cm}} \times \underline{\hspace{1cm}}$$

$$= \underline{\hspace{1cm}}$$

2 12^3

$$= \underline{\hspace{1cm}} \times \underline{\hspace{1cm}} \times \underline{\hspace{1cm}}$$

$$= \underline{\hspace{1cm}} \times \underline{\hspace{1cm}}$$

$$= \underline{\hspace{1cm}}$$

Write each expression as a power.

3 $4 \times 4 \times 4$

$$\underline{\hspace{1cm}}$$

4 $7 \times 7 \times 7$

$$\underline{\hspace{1cm}}$$

Evaluate each expression.

5 $8^3 - 3^3$

$$= \underline{\hspace{1cm}} \times \underline{\hspace{1cm}} \times \underline{\hspace{1cm}} - \underline{\hspace{1cm}} \times \underline{\hspace{1cm}} \times \underline{\hspace{1cm}}$$

$$= \underline{\hspace{1cm}} - \underline{\hspace{1cm}}$$

$$= \underline{\hspace{1cm}}$$

6 $2^3 + 1^3$

$$= \underline{\hspace{1cm}} \times \underline{\hspace{1cm}} \times \underline{\hspace{1cm}} + \underline{\hspace{1cm}} \times \underline{\hspace{1cm}} \times \underline{\hspace{1cm}}$$

$$= \underline{\hspace{1cm}} + \underline{\hspace{1cm}}$$

$$= \underline{\hspace{1cm}}$$

You know how to find the square or cube of a number. You can also find the **square root** of a number. The square root is one of two equal factors whose square is the given number.

$9 \times 9 = 81$, so the square root of 81 is 9.

The symbol for the **principal square root** or positive number is $\sqrt{\ }$.

Since $9 \times 9 = 81$, then $\sqrt{81} = 9$.

> I get it! I need to find the factor which, when multiplied by itself, is equal to the number inside the square root symbol.

You can find the **cube root** of a number as well. The cube root is one of three equal factors whose cube is the given number.

$4 \times 4 \times 4 = 64$, so the cube root of 64 is 4.

The symbol for cube root is $\sqrt[3]{\ }$.

Since $4 \times 4 \times 4 = 64$, then $\sqrt[3]{64} = 4$.

> For a cube root, I need to find the number which, when used as a factor three times, is equal to the number inside the cube root symbol.

Words to Know

square root	principal square root	cube root
one of two equal factors of a number whose square is equal to that number	the nonnegative (positive) square root of a number	one of three equal factors of a number whose cube is equal to that number
The square root of 81 is 9.		The cube root of 64 is 4.

DISCUSS Anna says that 4 is both a square number and a square root. Explain what she means.

LESSON LINK

PLUG IN	**POWER UP**	**GO!**
You can find the square of a number by multiplying it by itself.	To find the cube of a number, you calculate the product of three equal factors.	I get it! I can use what I know about finding the square and cube of a number to find square roots and cube roots.
$10^2 = 10 \times 10 = 100$	$10^3 = 10 \times 10 \times 10 = 1{,}000$	

WORK TOGETHER

You can use dot paper to model square roots.

> I see! I can use dot paper to find a square root of a number by drawing a square with the area of that number. The square root is the length of each side.

- The large square contains 16 smaller square units.

- Each side, *s*, of the blue square is 4 units long.

- The area of a square is s^2 or $s \times s$. For this square, $s \times s = 4 \times 4 = 16$. $s = \sqrt{16} = 4$.

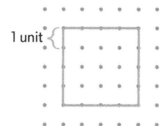

1 unit

1 square unit

$A = 16$ square units

$s = 4$ units

Dot Paper can be found on p. 211.

A You can use dot paper to find a square root.

DO Evaluate $\sqrt{36}$.

1 On dot paper, draw a square that has an area of 36 square units.

2 Find the length of each side of the square.

3 Write the square root.

Each side of the square is _____ units long.

The model shows that $\sqrt{\boxed{}} =$ _____.

B You can use reasoning to find a cube root.

DO Evaluate $\sqrt[3]{125}$.

> I see! I list the cube numbers and work backward to find the cube root of a number.

1 Understand the problem.

2 List the cubes of integers until you find a product of 125.

3 Find $\sqrt[3]{125}$.

Find the number that, when used as a factor _____ times, has a product of _____.

$1^3 = 1 \times 1 \times 1 =$ _____

$2^3 =$ _____ $\times$ _____ $\times$ _____ $=$ _____

$3^3 =$ _____ $\times$ _____ $\times$ _____ $=$ _____

$4^3 =$ _____ $\times$ _____ $\times$ _____ $=$ _____

$5^3 =$ _____ $\times$ _____ $\times$ _____ $=$ _____

Because _____ $\times$ _____ $\times$ _____ $= 125$, $\sqrt[3]{\text{_____}} =$ _____.

 DISCUSS You can use a square to model square numbers and square roots. What figure can you use to model cube numbers and cube roots? How do you know?

PRACTICE

Use dot paper to model and find each square root.

1 Find $\sqrt{9}$.

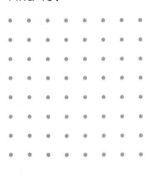

$\sqrt{9} =$ _____

2 Find $\sqrt{25}$.

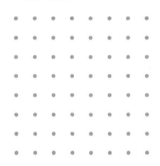

$\sqrt{25} =$ _____

Use reasoning to find each root.

3 Find $\sqrt{49}$.

_____ $\times$ _____ $= 49$

$\sqrt{49} =$ _____

4 Find $\sqrt{121}$.

_____ $\times$ _____ $= 121$

$\sqrt{121} =$ _____

HINT
Make a list of the first ten square numbers and cube numbers to solve these problems.

5 Find $\sqrt[3]{27}$.

_____ $\times$ _____ $\times$ _____ $= 27$

$\sqrt[3]{27} =$ _____

6 Find $\sqrt[3]{216}$.

_____ $\times$ _____ $\times$ _____ $= 216$

$\sqrt[3]{216} =$ _____

7 Find $\sqrt{64}$.

$\sqrt{64} =$ _____

8 Find $\sqrt[3]{64}$.

$\sqrt[3]{64} =$ _____

Complete each number sentence.

9 $\sqrt{\boxed{}} = 12$

10 $\sqrt[3]{\boxed{}} = 2$

11 $\sqrt{\boxed{}} = 10$

12 $\sqrt[3]{\boxed{}} = 1$

Solve.

13 Evaluate each square root to find the lengths of the sides of this triangle.

$AB = $ _____ m, $BC = $ _____ m, $CA = $ _____ m

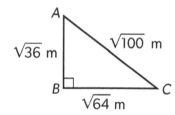

To find the square root of 36, I can ask myself: "What number times itself equals 36"?

14 What is the length of each side of the square?   _____ cm

$A = 121 \text{ cm}^2$

15 What is the length of each edge of the cube?   _____ cm

$V = 1,000 \text{ cm}^3$

 Critique Reasoning

Ben says, "I am thinking of a whole number whose cube root is the same as its square root. What is my number?" Raj says he can think of two possible answers. What numbers is Raj thinking of?

I remember! The whole numbers include the positive integers and 0.

PROBLEM SOLVING

GIFT BOXES

READ

The owner of a gift shop wants to order boxes that have a volume of 729 cubic inches. If she selects a cube-shaped box, what will the dimensions of the box be?

PLAN

• What is the problem asking you to find?

　　You need to find the dimensions of the box shaped like a _____.

• What do you need to know to solve the problem?

　　You need to know that the length, width, and height of a cube are equal.

　　You can use the _____ of the cube-shaped box to find its _____.

• How can you solve the problem?

　　Use the formula $V = s^3$ and what you know about _____ roots to solve the problem.

SOLVE

Write the formula.

Substitute the volume for V.

Find the cube root to solve for s.

Think: what number cubed equals 729?

_____ × _____ × _____ = _____

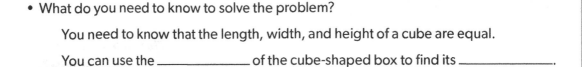

$$V = s^3$$
$$\underline{\hphantom{xxxx}} = s^3$$
$$\sqrt[3]{\boxed{\hphantom{xxx}}} = s$$
$$\underline{\hphantom{xxxx}} = s$$

CHECK

Find the volume of a right rectangular prism where each edge length is _____ inches.

The volume should be equal to _____ cubic inches.

The volume of a right rectangular prism is the product of the area of the base, B, and the height, h.

The base of a cube is a square.

$B = (\underline{\hphantom{xxx}})^2 = \underline{\hphantom{xxx}} \times \underline{\hphantom{xxx}} = \underline{\hphantom{xxx}}$

> I remember! A cube is one type of right rectangular prism.

The volume of the prism is the product of the base and the height.

$V = B \times h = \underline{\hphantom{xxx}} \times \underline{\hphantom{xxx}} = \underline{\hphantom{xxx}}$

The dimensions of the box are _____ inches by _____ inches by _____ inches.

Don't forget to include units for side lengths.

PRACTICE

Use the problem-solving steps to help you.

Find the square root or cube root to solve each problem.

1 The area of the square rug in Milo's classroom is 16 square feet. What is length of each side of the rug?

CHECKLIST
- [ ] READ
- [ ] PLAN
- [ ] SOLVE
- [ ] CHECK

2 A fish tank in a restaurant is shaped like a cube. It can hold 27 cubic feet of water. What is its height?

CHECKLIST
- [ ] READ
- [ ] PLAN
- [ ] SOLVE
- [ ] CHECK

3 Marsha stores her school supplies in a cube-shaped box with a volume of 512 in.^{3}. She sees that each face of the box is a square. What is the length of each edge of the top of the box?

CHECKLIST
- [ ] READ
- [ ] PLAN
- [ ] SOLVE
- [ ] CHECK

Scientific Notation

PLUG IN · Expressing Magnitude

If you wanted to describe how many times as great a number a is than the number b, you can use multiplication. To show that a is 6 times as great as b, write $a = 6b$.

How do you show that 24 is 8 times as great as 3? Write: $24 = 8 \times 3$

So this is a new way to compare numbers.

You can also use division to describe how many times as great a number c is than d. To show that c is 5 times as great as d, write $c \div d = 5$.

How do show that 10 is 5 times as great as 2? Write: $10 \div 2 = 5$

I get it! I can divide to find how many times as great one number is as another.

You can express how numbers are related in problem situations.

Sarah ran 42 miles this week and 21 miles last week. How many times as great as 21 is 42?

$$\begin{array}{r} 2 \\ 21\overline{)42} \\ -42 \\ \hline 0 \end{array}$$

I see! Sarah ran two times as far this week as last week.

DISCUSS Minnie says the word "times" is used to describe multiplication. She asks how this is related to questions where she is asked "how many times as great" one number is as another. What would you tell her?

A You can use division to find how many times as great one number is as another.

DO How many times as great as 25 is 250? How many times as great as 10 is 250? How many times as great as 5 is 250?

1 Divide.

$250 \div 25 =$ _____ $250 \div 10 =$ _____ $250 \div 5 =$ _____

2 Express how many times as great one number is as another.

250 is _____ times as great as 25.

250 is _____ times as great as 10.

250 is _____ times as great as 5.

I see! The number of times one number is as great as another can be less than 1.

 B You can express how many times as great one number is as another.

DO

How many times as great as 100 is 25? How many times as great as 100 is 50?

1 Divide.

$25 \div 100 =$ _____ $50 \div 100 =$ _____

2 Express how many times as great one number is as another.

25 is _____ times as great as 100.

50 is _____ times as great as 100.

C You can solve problems using number comparisons.

DO

Aiden sold 30 coupon books for a fund-raiser. Jaxon sold 4 times as many coupon books as Aiden. How many coupon books did Jaxon sell?

1 Identify the given values.

Aiden sold _____ coupon books.

2 Write a multiplication or division equation for the comparison.

Jaxon sold _____ times as many as Aiden.

_____ × _____ = _____

Jaxon sold _____ coupon books.

 DISCUSS

Alexandra visited the same number of web pages today as her sister. She said, "I've visited one times as many web pages as you today." Does this statement make sense?

PRACTICE

Solve.

1 How many times as great as 9 is 36?

_____

2 How many times as great as 7 is 105?

_____

3 How many times as great as 30 is 180?

_____

4 How many times as great as 50 is 5?

_____

5 An art teacher has 63 erasers. A math teacher has 21 erasers. How many times as great is the art teacher's number of erasers as the math teacher's?

_____

6 One car dealer has 72 cars on her lot. Another car dealer has 36 cars on her lot. How many times as great is the first dealer's number of cars as the second dealer's?

_____

7 A builder uses 36 tiles for the kitchen floor and 9 tiles for the bathroom floor. How many times as great is the number of tiles for the kitchen floor as for the bathroom floor?

_____

8 A university has 3 vans to transport fans from the parking lot to the basketball arena. There are 75 times as many fans as there are vans. How many fans need to be transported?

_____

Converting Between Scientific Notation and Standard Form

A number in **scientific notation** is the product of a factor greater than or equal to 1 and less than 10, and a power of ten.

$$3 \times 10^9$$

To convert a number in scientific notation to standard form, expand the power of 10 and multiply it by the other factor.

$$5 \times 10^8 = 5 \times 100,000,000$$
$$= 500,000,000$$

To convert a number in standard form to scientific notation, first move the decimal point to form the factor equal to or greater than 1 and less than 10. Then use the number of places the decimal point moves as the power of 10.

$$0.000026 = 000002.6 \times 10^{-5}$$
$$340,000 = 3.40000 \times 10^5$$

I see! Scientific notation is a way to write a number using a multiplication expression.

So scientific notation lets me write a number with many zeros between the decimal point and a nonzero digit in an equivalent form.

I see! Numbers greater than or equal to 10 have positive exponents. Numbers less than 1 have negative exponents.

Words to Know

scientific notation
a way to express numbers using a multiplication expression in which the first factor, the coefficient, is a number that is greater than or equal to 1 and less than 10, and the second factor is a power of 10

$$3 \times 10^4 = 3 \times 10,000 = 30,000$$
$$0.025 = 2.5 \times 10^{-2}$$

DISCUSS

Marcus wants to write 50,000 using scientific notation. He writes 50×10^3. Is he correct? Explain.

A You can write numbers in scientific notation.

DO

Write 53,000 in scientific notation.

1. Move the decimal point to form the factor greater than or equal to 1 and less than 10.

☐ . ☐ 000

2. Count the number of places the decimal point moved.

The decimal point moved ___ places.

3. Write this number as the exponent for the power of 10.

$10^{☐}$

4. Write the first factor and the power of 10 as a multiplication expression.

$☐ . ☐ \times 10^{☐}$

B You can write numbers in scientific notation in standard form.

DO Write 1.81×10^{-6} in standard form.

❶ Determine the location of the decimal point based on the exponent of the power of 10.

❷ Write the number in standard form.

The exponent of the power of 10 is _____.

The decimal point will be _____ places to the _____.

_____

DISCUSS Ashton says if he wrote 3.1×10^{-3} in standard form, it would be a negative number. How would you explain his mistake?

PRACTICE

Rewrite each number in standard form.

❶ 5×10^6

_____

❷ 3×10^{-10}

_____

❸ 6.5×10^{-3}

_____

❹ 7.7×10^{-4}

_____

❺ 9.7×10^9

_____

❻ 8×10^7

_____

Rewrite each number in scientific notation.

❼ 0.000000001

_____

❽ 40,000,000,000

_____

❾ 0.00000098

_____

❿ 900,000,000

_____

⓫ 0.00000000041

_____

⓬ 0.00000089

_____

You can compare numbers written in scientific notation.

The library printer holds about 4×10^3 sheets of paper. The office printer holds about 2×10^2 sheets of paper. How many times the number of sheets of paper is held by the library printer as is held by the office printer?

$$(4 \times 10^3) \div (2 \times 10^2)$$

$$4 \div 2 = 2$$

$$10^3 \div 10^2 = 10^1$$

$$2 \times 10^1 = 2 \times 10 = 20$$

1. Write an expression for the number of sheets of paper the library printer holds divided by the number of sheets of paper the office printer holds.

2. Divide the coefficients.

3. Divide the powers of 10.

4. Multiply the quotient of the coefficients by the quotient of the powers of 10.

> I see! To divide exponents with the same base, I raise the base to the power that is the difference of the exponents. $10^3 \div 10^2 = 10^{(3-2)} = 10^1 = 10$

The library printer holds 20 times as many sheets of paper as the office printer.

DISCUSS Explain how you would multiply two numbers that are written in scientific notation.

LESSON LINK

PLUG IN	POWER UP	GO!
You can use division to compare numbers.	**You can use scientific notation to express very large or very small quantities.**	I get it! I can use what I've learned to work with numbers written in scientific notation!
How many times as great as 9 is 90?	$2.9 \times 10^{-3} = 0.0029$	
$90 \div 9 = 10$, so 90 is 10 times as great as 9.	$7 \times 10^7 = 70{,}000{,}000$	

WORK TOGETHER

I remember! To multiply exponents with the same base, raise the base to the power that is the sum of the exponents!

Multiply the coefficients and the powers of 10 to find the product of scientific notation.

$$(7 \times 10^{-6}) \cdot (2.5 \times 10^4)$$

- Find the product of the coefficients.

$$7 \times 2.5 = 17.5$$

- Find the product of the powers of 10.

$$10^{-6} \times 10^4 = 10^{-2}$$

- If necessary, rewrite the product in scientific notation.

$$17.5 \times 10^{-2} = 1.75 \times 10^{-1}$$

A You can multiply numbers that are written in scientific notation.

DO Multiply $(5.3 \times 10^{12}) \cdot (2 \times 10^{-4})$.

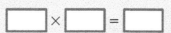

❶ Find the product of the coefficients.

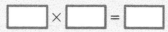

❷ Find the product of the powers of 10.

❸ Write the products as a multiplication expression. $(5.3 \times 10^{12}) \cdot (2 \times 10^{-4}) = $ _____

❹ Write the product in scientific notation. $(5.3 \times 10^{12}) \cdot (2 \times 10^{-4}) = $ _____

I see that the product of the coefficients is already greater than or equal to 1 and less than 10.

B You can divide numbers that are written in scientific notation.

DO Divide $(7.2 \times 10^{-4}) \div (3.2 \times 10^{-9})$.

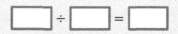

❶ Find the quotient of the coefficients.

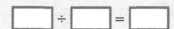

❷ Find the quotient of the powers of 10.

❸ Write the quotient in scientific notation.

$$(7.2 \times 10^{-4}) \div (3.2 \times 10^{-9}) = \text{_____}$$

I remember. There are 1,000 grams in 1 kilogram.

DISCUSS Kiara needs to write 7.5×10^6 grams as kilograms. How could she do that?

PRACTICE

Find each product or quotient.

1 $(6 \times 10^{-7}) \cdot (4.5 \times 10^8)$

The product of coefficients: _____ × _____ = _____

The product of powers of 10: _____ × _____ = _____

Write answer in scientific notation: _____

REMEMBER
The coefficient must be ≥ 1 and < 10.

2 $(9 \times 10^5) \div (1.5 \times 10^{-5})$

The quotient of coefficients: _____ ÷ _____ = _____

The quotient of powers of 10: _____ ÷ _____ = _____

Write answer in scientific notation: _____

HINT
Subtract exponents when dividing powers of 10.

3 $(3.9 \times 10^{-2}) \div (3 \times 10^6)$

The quotient of coefficients: _____ ÷ _____ = _____

The quotient of powers of 10: _____ ÷ _____ = _____

Write answer in scientific notation: _____

4 $(8.5 \times 10^{-6}) \cdot (1.6 \times 10^1)$

The product of coefficients: _____ × _____ = _____

The product of powers of 10: _____ × _____ = _____

Write answer in scientific notation: _____

5 $(6.8 \times 10^{-10}) \cdot (2.2 \times 10^{-4})$

The product of coefficients: _____ × _____ = _____

The product of powers of 10: _____ × _____ = _____

Write answer in scientific notation: _____

6 $(7.2 \times 10^3) \div (5 \times 10^8)$

The quotient of coefficients: _____ ÷ _____ = _____

The quotient of powers of 10: _____ ÷ _____ = _____

Write answer in scientific notation: _____

Find each product or quotient. Write your answer in scientific notation.

7 $(3.5 \times 10^2) \cdot (5.8 \times 10^5)$

_____

8 $(5.4 \times 10^{-3}) \div (4.5 \times 10^3)$

_____

9 $(3.9 \times 10^2) \div (2.6 \times 10^{-9})$

_____

10 $(3.4 \times 10^{10}) \cdot (2.5 \times 10^{-3})$

_____

First, determine which operation to use to solve the problem.

Solve.

11 Alana bought 8.5×10^3 red beads and 1.7×10^3 white beads to make bracelets for her friends. How many times the number of white beads is the number of red beads she bought?

_____

12 Corey estimated that he takes about 1.8×10^4 steps each day. About how many steps will he take in 180 days? Write the answer in scientific notation.

_____

 Reasoning

I remember! I need to divide to find how many times as great one number is as another.

Chloe bought 1.2×10^2 paper plates and 5.04×10^3 napkins for her restaurant. She wondered, "How many times as great as the number of paper plates I bought was the number of napkins?"

Explain how you know if the exponent to the answer will be positive or negative.

How many times as great as the number of paper plates Chloe bought was the number of napkins?

PROBLEM SOLVING

SWIMMINGLY WELL

READ

A swimming pool holds 1.92×10^6 milligrams of chlorine and 6.4×10^5 liters of water. How many milligrams of chlorine are in 1 liter of water?

PLAN

- What is the problem asking you to find?

    You need to find the number of _____

    in _____ .

- What do you need to know to solve the problem?

    How many milligrams of chlorine are in the pool? _____

    How many liters of water are in the pool? _____

- How can you find the solution? _____

    _____

SOLVE

$(1.92 \times 10^6) \div (6.4 \times 10^5)$

The quotient of coefficients: __**1.92**__ $\div$ __**6.4**__ = _____

The quotient of powers of 10: _____ $\div$ _____ = _____

Write the answer in scientific notation: _____

CHECK

Multiply your answer by 6.4×10^5 liters. The product will be the number of milligrams of chlorine in the pool.

$(3 \times 10^0) \cdot (6.4 \times 10^5)$

The product of coefficients: _____ $\times$ _____ = _____

The product of powers of 10: _____ $\times$ _____ = _____

Write the answer in scientific notation: _____

> Any nonzero base raised to the power of 0 is equal to 1.

There are _____ milligrams of chlorine for every 1 liter of water.

PRACTICE

Use the problem-solving steps to help you. Write the answer in standard form and in scientific notation.

Any number raised to the first power is equal to that number.

1 The school collected 3.3×10^4 pounds of paper and 1.5×10^3 pounds aluminum to recycle. How many times the amount of aluminum collected was the amount of paper collected?

CHECKLIST
- [ ] READ
- [ ] PLAN
- [ ] SOLVE
- [ ] CHECK

2 Malcolm sent 1.2×10^3 text messages last month. At this rate, about how many text messages will Malcolm send in 1 year?

CHECKLIST
- [ ] READ
- [ ] PLAN
- [ ] SOLVE
- [ ] CHECK

3 How long would it take a rocket to travel 4×10^6 miles if its speed was 1.6×10^3 miles per hour?

To find the time of a trip, I divide the distance by the speed.

CHECKLIST
- [ ] READ
- [ ] PLAN
- [ ] SOLVE
- [ ] CHECK

Comparing Proportional Relationships

PLUG IN   Unit Rate and Slope of a Line

A **unit rate** is a ratio that compares a quantity to 1.

x	y	$\frac{y}{x}$
1	3	$\frac{3}{1}$
2	6	$\frac{6}{2} = \frac{3}{1}$
3	9	$\frac{9}{3} = \frac{3}{1}$
4	12	$\frac{12}{4} = \frac{3}{1}$
5	15	$\frac{15}{5} = \frac{3}{1}$

In this table, the unit rate is $\frac{3}{1}$.

> I see! When written as a fraction, the unit rate has a denominator of 1.

The **slope** of a line is a ratio of the change in its *y*-coordinates (the *rise*) to the change in its corresponding *x*-coordinates (the *run*).

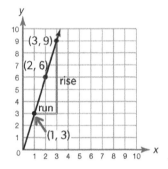

By the points (1, 3) and (3, 9), the slope of the line is $\frac{9-3}{3-1} = \frac{6}{2} = \frac{3}{1}$.

> I get it! The unit rate and the slope are equivalent!

Words to Know

unit rate
a ratio that compares a quantity to 1

slope
a ratio of the change in y-coordinates (*rise*) of a graph to the change in corresponding x-coordinates (*run*)

DISCUSS   Review the table and graph. Which points on the line can you use to calculate its slope?

A You can find the slope to determine the unit rate of a proportional relationship.

DO   The graph represents a proportional relationship. What is the unit rate of the graph?

1 Use the labeled points to find the slope of the line.

2 Write the slope as a ratio in simplest form.

3 The unit rate is equivalent to the slope.

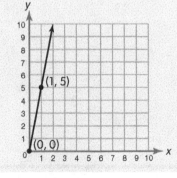

$\frac{\square - \square}{\square - \square} = \frac{\square}{\square}$

The unit rate is $\frac{\square}{\square}$.

B You can find the unit rate for a real-world situation.

This graph represents the total cost of cheese based on the number of pounds purchased. This relationship is proportional.

Find the cost per pound, or unit rate.

① Pick two points on the line and find the slope.

② Write the slope as a ratio in simplest form.

③ The unit rate is equivalent to the slope of a proportional relationship.

> Make sure you subtract the x-values in the same order that you subtract the y-values from the two points.

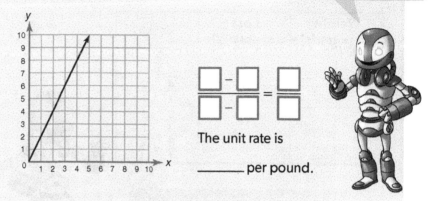

The unit rate is _____ per pound.

PRACTICE

Find the unit rate of each proportional relationship.

1

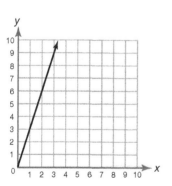

The unit rate is _____.

2

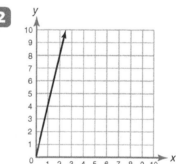

The unit rate is _____.

3

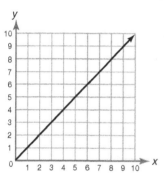

The unit rate is _____.

4

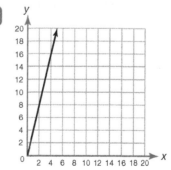

The unit rate is _____.

Graphing a Proportional Relationship

In a proportional relationship, the ratios of the quantities compared are the same.

Weight (in pounds)	Cost (in dollars)	Ratio
1	2	$\frac{2}{1}$
2	4	$\frac{4}{2} = \frac{2}{1}$
3	6	$\frac{6}{3} = \frac{2}{1}$
4	8	$\frac{8}{4} = \frac{2}{1}$

You can use the values in the table as coordinate pairs to create a graph of the proportional relationship.

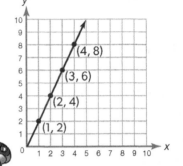

I see! Since each of the ratios can be written as $\frac{2}{1}$, the table shows a proportional relationship.

I remember! The graph of a proportional relationship is a line that passes through the origin.

DISCUSS Ming bought 10 pounds of meat for $30. If this relationship between cost and weight were graphed, how would she know if the relationship was proportional?

A You can identify a proportional relationship by graphing a table of data.

DO Graph the relationship shown in the table.

1 Plot each point.

2 Connect the points with a line.

3 Determine if the line passes through the origin.

x	y
1	4
2	8
3	12
4	16
5	20

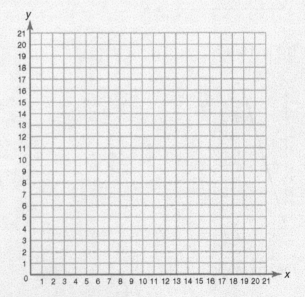

The line includes the origin. The table represents a proportional relationship.

B You can graph a proportional relationship using a verbal description.

DO

Tamara earns $8 per hour for babysitting. Complete the table and graph this relationship.

1 Complete the table.

2 Graph the data by plotting each point.

3 Draw a line that includes each point.

Hours	Amount Earned (in dollars)
1	
2	
3	
4	
5	

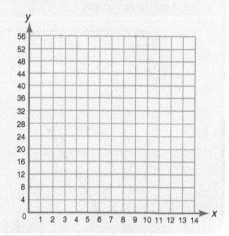

DISCUSS

Oliver knows the graph above represents a proportional relationship. He wonders if a line parallel to this graph through (1, 9) is a proportional relationship as well. How would you explain the answer to him?

You can sketch the line Oliver is thinking of to help you.

PRACTICE

Graph each proportional relationship.

1

x	y
2	1
4	2
6	3
8	4
10	5

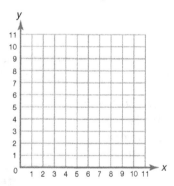

2

x	y
0	0
1	5
2	10
3	15
4	20

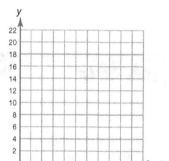

3

x	y
1	1
2	2
3	3
4	4
5	5

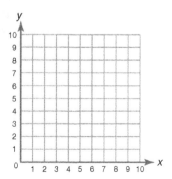

4

x	y
3	1
6	2
9	3
12	4
15	5

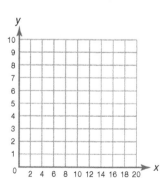

Comparing Proportional Relationships

Proportional relationships can be represented using a table or graph.

x	2	4	6	8	10
y	3	6	9	12	15

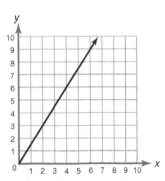

The unit rate is $\frac{1.5}{1}$.

The slope is $\frac{3}{2}$ or 1.5.

Another way to represent a proportional relationship is with an equation.

All proportional relationships have the form $y = kx$, where k is any nonzero number and represents the unit rate (or slope).

The equation is $y = 1.5x$.

I know this is a proportional relationship because the ratio $\frac{y}{x}$ is constant in the table, and because the graph is a line that passes through the origin.

I see! To find the unit rate of a proportional relationship expressed as an equation, I can just look at the coefficient of x.

DISCUSS

Compare the proportional relationship $y = 3x$ to $y = 1.5x$. Which has a greater unit rate? How do you know?

LESSON LINK

PLUG IN

You can determine the unit rate of a proportional relationship by finding the constant ratio $\frac{y}{x}$ in a table of values or the slope of its graph.

x	1	2	3	4	5
y	4	8	12	16	20

POWER UP

You can graph a proportional relationship, which is represented by a line that passes through the origin.

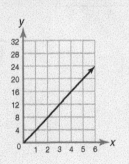

GO!

I see! I can compare proportional relationships represented as graphs, tables, or equations by finding the unit rate.

WORK TOGETHER

You can compare two proportional relationships by finding their unit rates.

- Find Sherine's unit rate.
- Find Devon's unit rate.
- Compare the unit rates.

Sherine and Devon each handed out flyers at a constant rate. Sherine made a table of the number of flyers she handed out, and Devon made a graph. Who handed out flyers at a greater rate?

> I see! The words "constant rate" let me know that these relationships are proportional.

Sherine's Table

Flyers Passed Out over Time

Hours	Flyers
0	0
1	7
2	14
3	21
4	28

Devon's Graph

Flyers Passed Out over Time

The unit rate is the change in quantity per unit of measure.

Sherine's rate $= \dfrac{\text{change in flyers}}{\text{change in hours}} = \dfrac{14 - 7 \text{ flyers}}{2 - 1 \text{ hours}} = \dfrac{7 \text{ flyers}}{1 \text{ hour}} = 7$ flyers per hour

The slope of a graph is equal to the unit rate.

$$\text{Slope} = \dfrac{\text{change in } y\text{-coordinates}}{\text{change in } x\text{-coordinates}}$$

Slope of Devon's graph $= \dfrac{15 - 10 \text{ flyers}}{3 - 2 \text{ hours}} = \dfrac{5 \text{ flyers}}{1 \text{ hour}} = 5$ flyers per hour

Sherine's rate is greater.

A You can compare proportional relationships that are represented in different ways.

DO

Dwayne used the equation $y = 3.25x$ to represent the total cost when buying x gallons of gasoline in City A. Dena created a table to represent the total cost when buying x gallons of gasoline in City B. Which city sells gasoline at a lower unit rate?

x	2	4	6	8	10
y	6.40	12.80	19.20	25.60	32.00
$\frac{y}{x}$					

1 Identify the unit rate for City A.   The equation $y = 3.25x$ represents City A.

2 Calculate the unit rate for City B.   The unit rate is _____.

3 Compare unit rates.   _____ > _____. City _____ sells gasoline at a lower unit rate.

DISCUSS

If you know the table of values for a proportional relationship, how could you express the relationship as an equation?

PRACTICE

Choose the proportional relationship with the greater unit rate.

1 The graph shows the number of shopping bags shipped to a bookstore each month.

Shopping Bags Shipped to Bookstore over Time

The bookstore also gets a shipment of 750 books every month.

Which item is delivered at a greater unit rate, shopping bags or books?

_____

2 The table shows the number of sea lions seen by tourists over time.

Sea Lion Sightings over Time

Hours	Number Seen
0	0
2	32
4	64
6	96

If the biologist saw 13 sea otters per hour, the animal that she saw at a greater rate is the

_____.

3 The graph shows the number of plums picked over time.

Fruit Harvest at Williams Orchards

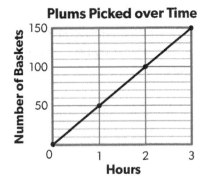

Plums Picked over Time

Peaches Picked over Time

Hours	Number of Baskets
0	0
2	126
4	252
6	378

The equation $y = 63x$ represents the number of peaches picked, y, in x hours.

The fruit picked at a greater rate is _____.

Choose the proportional relationship with the greater rate.

4 The table and graph show the number of food items sold over time at basketball games.

Food Sold at Basketball Games

Peanuts Sold over Time

Hot Dogs Sold over Time

Hours	Number Sold
$1\frac{1}{2}$	66
2	88
$2\frac{1}{2}$	110

The food sold at a greater rate is _____.

Determine the greater rate in each situation.

I can compare rates more easily if I show the information in these problems in a table.

5 Hector raked 1 bag of leaves in 0.5 hours and 3 bags in 1.5 hours. Blaine raked 3 bags of leaves in 1 hour and 6 bags in 2 hours. Who raked leaves at a greater rate? _____

6 A waiter poured 2 gallons of coffee in 2 hours and 6 gallons of coffee in 6 hours. He also poured 1.5 gallons of tea in 3 hours and 2.5 gallons of tea in 5 hours. Which drink did the waiter pour at a greater rate? _____

DISCUSS

Comparing Relationships

I remember! I have to find a constant ratio $\frac{y}{x}$ to show a relationship is proportional.

Luis folded 8 shirts in 10 minutes and 18 shirts in 20 minutes. Carly folded 3 shirts in 5 minutes and 9 shirts in 15 minutes.

Determine if the number of shirts Luis folds per minute represents a proportional relationship. Explain your answer.

What is Carly's unit rate written as a decimal? _____ shirts per minute

Can you compare Luis and Carly's unit rates for folding clothes?

PROBLEM SOLVING

FASTER FAUCET

READ

Which faucet should Oliver use to fill the dog bathtub as quickly as possible?

Kitchen Faucet Flow over Time

Minutes	Gallons
0	0
2	4
3	6

Bathroom Faucet Flow over Time

PLAN

• You need to find the faucet with the _____ flow rate.

• You need to know the flow rate of both faucets in _____ per minute.

• Use the table to find unit rate, and use the graph to find slope.

SOLVE

Find the flow rate of the kitchen faucet.

$$\frac{\text{change in gallons}}{\text{change in minutes}} = \frac{\boxed{6} - \boxed{4} \text{ gallons}}{\boxed{} - \boxed{} \text{ minutes}} = \frac{\boxed{} \text{ gallons}}{\boxed{} \text{ minute}}$$

Find the flow rate of the bathroom faucet.

$$\frac{\text{change in gallons}}{\text{change in minutes}} = \frac{\boxed{} - \boxed{} \text{ gallons}}{\boxed{} - \boxed{} \text{ minutes}} = \frac{\boxed{} \text{ gallons}}{\boxed{} \text{ minute}}$$

> The faucet with the faster flow rate will fill up the tub faster.

CHECK

Graph the flow for both faucets. Include a key. Compare the slopes.

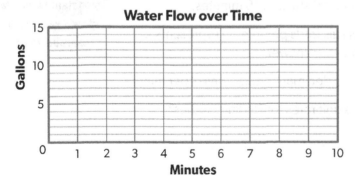

Water Flow over Time

Which faucet should Oliver use? _____

PRACTICE

Use the problem-solving steps to help you.

To find how long it takes the faster runner to run 6 laps, I multiply the unit rate by the number of laps!

1 Keisha and Fatima are running laps around the track.

Keisha's Running Times

Laps	Minutes
0.5	0.8
1.5	2.4
2	3.2

Fatima's Running Times

Who runs at a faster rate? How long would it take the faster runner to run 6 laps?

CHECKLIST
- [ ] READ
- [ ] PLAN
- [ ] SOLVE
- [ ] CHECK

2 Ty and Jamal are making sandwiches together. Ty can make 3 sandwiches in 2 minutes and 6 in 4 minutes. Jamal can make 1 sandwiches in 2 minutes and 2 in 4 minutes.

How many will they have made together in 10 minutes? How many will each have made?

I can use the unit rate to find the number of sandwiches in a given time.

CHECKLIST
- [ ] READ
- [ ] PLAN
- [ ] SOLVE
- [ ] CHECK

3 The number of dog walkers and joggers in a park are shown in the table and graph below.

Joggers Counted over Time

Hours	Number of Joggers
0	0
1	12
3	36
5	60

The number of dog walkers and joggers continues to increase at the same rate throughout the day. Will there be more joggers or dog walkers at hour 8? How many will there be of each at hour 8?

CHECKLIST
- [ ] READ
- [ ] PLAN
- [ ] SOLVE
- [ ] CHECK

43

PLUG IN Finding the Slope of a Line

The **slope** of a line is the ratio of the change in the y-values to the change in the corresponding x-values.

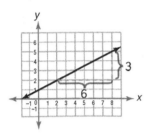

$$\text{Slope} = \frac{\text{change in }y\text{-values}}{\text{change in }x\text{-values}}$$

$$= \frac{5-2}{8-2} = \frac{3}{6} = \frac{1}{2}$$

I see! I choose two coordinate pairs and then divide the difference of the y-values by the difference of the corresponding x-values.

The **y-intercept** is where a line crosses the y-axis.

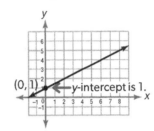

(0, 1) y-intercept is 1.

The y-intercept is the y-coordinate of the point where the line intersects the y-axis.

The equation of a line can be written in the form $y = mx + b$, where the slope of the line is m, and the y-intercept is b.

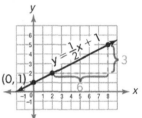

$y = \frac{1}{2}x + 1$

(0, 1)

I get it! The slope is $m = \frac{1}{2}$, and the y-intercept is $b = 1$, so the equation of the line is $y = \frac{1}{2}x + 1$.

Words to Know

slope
a ratio of the change in y-coordinates (*rise*) of a graph to the change in corresponding x-coordinates (*run*)

y-intercept
the y-coordinate of the point at which a line crosses the y-axis

DISCUSS Will the slope of the line through the points (1, 6) and (7, −2) be positive or negative? How do you know?

A You can use the slope formula $m = \frac{y_2 - y_1}{x_2 - x_1}$ to find the slope of a line.

DO Find the slope of the line through points (5, 1) and (−4, 3).

1 Choose (x_1, y_1) and (x_2, y_2).

2 Write the slope formula. Substitute for x_1, x_2, y_1, and y_2.

3 Subtract. Simplify, if possible.

$(x_1, y_1) = (5, 1)$ $(x_2, y_2) = \left(\boxed{}, \boxed{}\right)$

$\text{slope} = \dfrac{y_2 - y_1}{x_2 - x_1} = \dfrac{3 - \boxed{}}{\boxed{} - 5} = \dfrac{\boxed{}}{\boxed{}}$

B You can use the equation of a line to find its slope and y-intercept.

DO Find the slope and y-intercept of the line with the equation $y = 3x + 2$.

① Compare the equation of the given line to $y = mx + b$.

$y = \boxed{}x + \boxed{}$

$y = m \cdot x + b$

② Identify the slope, m, and the y-intercept, b.

$m = \boxed{}$

$b = \boxed{}$

The slope of the line is _____.

The y-intercept of the line is _____.

DISCUSS Why do you think the slope of a vertical line is described as "undefined"? Explain by computing the slope of the vertical line through points (2, 6) and (2, −3).

PRACTICE

Find the slope of the line that contains the given points.

1 (2, 1) and (4, 2)

$m = \dfrac{2 - \boxed{}}{\boxed{} - 2} = \dfrac{\boxed{}}{\boxed{}}$

2 (1, 3) and (5, 6)

$m = \dfrac{\boxed{} - \boxed{}}{\boxed{} - \boxed{}} = \dfrac{\boxed{}}{\boxed{}}$

Find the slope and y-intercept of each line.

3

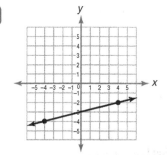

slope = _____

y-intercept = _____

4

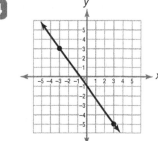

slope = _____

y-intercept = _____

5 $y = \frac{1}{2}x + 5$

slope = _____

y-intercept = _____

6 $y = -2x + 3$

slope = _____

y-intercept = _____

You can write the equation of a line from its graph using the form $y = mx + b$.

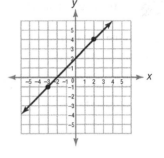

① **Find the slope.** Choose two points on the line, and use the slope formula to calculate the slope. Using the points $(-3, -1)$ and $(2, 4)$:

$$m = \frac{\text{change in } y\text{-values}}{\text{change in } x\text{-values}}$$

$$= \frac{y_2 - y_1}{x_2 - x_1}$$

$$= \frac{4 - (-1)}{2 - (-3)}$$

$$= \frac{5}{5}$$

$$= 1$$

② **Find the y-intercept.** Identify where the line crosses the y-axis.

The line crosses the y-axis at $(0, 2)$.

The y-intercept is 2.

③ **Substitute the slope, *m*, and the y-intercept, *b*, in the equation $y = mx + b$.**

$y = mx + b$

$y = x + 2$ is an equation for the line.

The x and y in the equation represent all the possible coordinate pairs of points on the line.

I see! If I know the slope and y-intercept of a line, then I can write an equation for the line.

 Does the slope change, depending on which point you assign as (x_1, y_1) or (x_2, y_2)? Explain.

A You can write the equation of a line if given the slope and y-intercept.

DO   What is the equation of a line that has a slope of 8 and a y-intercept of -2.

① Identify m and b.

② Substitute the slope, m, and the y-intercept, b, in the equation $y = mx + b$.

③ Write the equation.

$m = $ _____

$b = $ _____

$y = mx + b$

$y = \boxed{}x + \boxed{}$

$y = $ _____

I remember! *m* stands for slope and *b* represents the y-intercept.

B You can write the equation of a line that passes through the origin.

DO

Write an equation for the line shown in the graph.

1 Choose two points on the line.

2 Find the slope. $m = \frac{y_2 - y_1}{x_2 - x_1}$

3 Identify the y-Intercept.

4 Write the equation. Simplify, if possible.

$(x_1, y_1) = (2, \boxed{})$

$(x_2, y_2) = (\boxed{}, -2)$

$m = \dfrac{\boxed{} - \boxed{}}{\boxed{} - \boxed{}} = \dfrac{\boxed{}}{\boxed{}}$

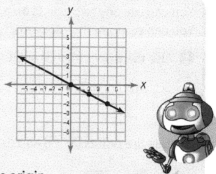

The line crosses the y-axis at the origin.

So $b = \boxed{}$.

$y = \dfrac{\boxed{}}{\boxed{}}x + \boxed{} = \dfrac{\boxed{}}{\boxed{}}x$

> I remember! The coordinates of the origin are represented by the point (0,0).

DISCUSS

Andrew says that he can use the form $y = b$ to write the equation for any horizontal line that passes through the point $(0, b)$. Is Andrew correct? Explain.

PRACTICE

Write the equation for the line.

1

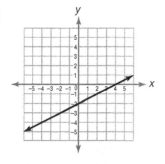

_____

2

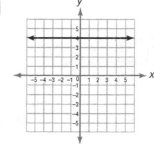

_____

> I remember! All horizontal lines have a slope of 0. That means $m = 0$ for all horizontal lines.

Write an equation of the line with the given slope and y-intercept.

3 slope = 3; y-intercept = 7

_____

4 slope = $\frac{-2}{5}$; y-intercept = −3

_____

Write an equation of the line that passes through the given points.

5 (0, 4) and (−5, 2)

_____

6 (0, 2) and (4, 6)

_____

47

You can use any two points on a line to find the slope of the line.
You can compare the slopes of two segments of the line to show this.

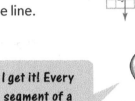

1 Use the points $(0, -3)$ and $(3, -1)$ to find the slope of the line.

$$m = \frac{-1 - (-3)}{3 - 0}$$

$$= \frac{2}{3}$$

2 Use the points $(3, -1)$ and $(9, 3)$ to find the slope of the line.

$$m = \frac{3 - (-1)}{9 - 3}$$

$$= \frac{4}{6}$$

$$= \frac{2}{3}$$

3 Compare the slopes.

$$\frac{2}{3} = \frac{2}{3}$$

The slopes are equal.

> I get it! Every segment of a line will have the same slope!

DISCUSS

Margarita looks at a table of x-y values and calculates the slope using one pair of points. She uses another pair of points and calculates a different slope. What can Margarita conclude about a graph of those points?

LESSON LINK

PLUG IN

You can find the slope and y-intercept of a line given any two points on the line, its graph, or its equation.

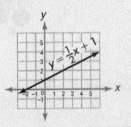

slope: $m = \frac{1}{2}$

y-intercept: $b = 1$

POWER UP

You can use the slope and y-intercept of a line to write an equation for the line.

Slope: $m = \frac{5}{8}$

y-intercept: $b = -2$

$$y = mx + b$$

$$y = \frac{5}{8}x + (-2)$$

$$= \frac{5}{8}x - 2$$

GO!

> I get it! I can investigate slope and y-intercept further to better understand the characteristics of lines!

WORK TOGETHER

Use two pairs of points to confirm the slope of a line.

- This line includes the points $(-1, 6)$, $(1, 2)$, $(2, 0)$, and $(5, -6)$.
- The slope between $(-1, 6)$ and $(1, 2)$ is $-\frac{4}{2}$, or -2.
- The slope between $(2, 0)$ and $(5, -6)$ is $\frac{-6}{3} = -\frac{2}{1}$, or -2.
- The slope of the line is the same with either pair of points.

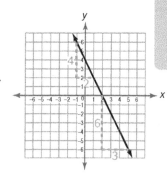

I could also use any other two pairs of points on this line to confirm the slope.

A You can use slope to check whether three points lie on the same line.

DO Determine if the points $(0, 6)$, $(3, 3)$, and $(6, -1)$ are on the same line.

1 Find the slope between any two of the three points.

2 Now find the slope between two other points.

3 Compare the slopes to determine if the points are on the same line.

Use $(0, 6)$ and $(3, 3)$.

$$m = \frac{\square - \square}{\square - \square} = \frac{\square}{\square} = \square$$

Use $(3, 3)$ and $(6, -1)$.

$$m = \frac{\square - \square}{\square - \square} = \frac{\square}{\square}$$

The three points _____ on the same line

because the slopes are _____.

B You can determine if two segments that share an endpoint are on the same line.

DO Determine if two segments, one with endpoints $(0, 2)$ and $(4, 3)$ and one with endpoints $(0, 2)$ and $(8, 4)$, lie along the same line.

1 Find the slope of the first segment.

2 Find the slope of the second segment.

3 Compare the slopes to determine if they are on the same line.

Use $(0, 2)$ and $(4, 3)$.

$$m = \frac{\square - \square}{\square - \square} = \frac{\square}{\square}$$

Now use $(0, 2)$ and $(8, 4)$.

$$m = \frac{\square - \square}{\square - \square} = \frac{\square}{\square} = \frac{\square}{\square}$$

The slopes are _____. The 3 points _____ on the same line.

DISCUSS Will a line segment that is part of a larger line segment always have the same slope as the larger line segment? Explain.

PRACTICE

Solve.

 Coordinate Grid can be found on p.213

1 A line segment has endpoints at (−2, 5) and (1, 4). Another line segment has endpoints at (1, 4) and (2, 7). Are the line segments parts of the same line?

Find the slope of the first line segment.

$$m = \frac{4 - \square}{\square - (-2)} = \frac{\square}{\square}$$

Find the slope of the second line segment.

$$m = \frac{\square - 4}{2 - \square} = \frac{\square}{\square} = \square$$

HINT
You can check your answer by graphing the segments on a coordinate grid.

Are the line segments on the same line? Explain.

_____

2 Choose two pairs of points on the line to show the slope of the line is the same.

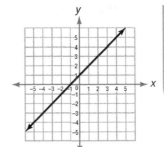

REMEMBER
Any two pairs of points on the line will show the same slope.

Use points (_____, _____) and (_____, _____).

$$m = \frac{\square - \square}{\square - \square} = \frac{\square}{\square} = \square$$

Now use points (_____, _____) and (_____, _____).

$$m = \frac{\square - \square}{\square - \square} = \frac{\square}{\square} = \square$$

Are the slopes the same? _____

3 Use the endpoints of two segments along this line to show that the slopes of the segments are the same.

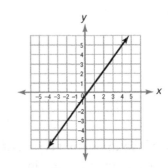

Are the slopes of the segments the same? _____

Solve.

4 Two line segments are part of the line $y = -\frac{1}{5}x + 10$. What is the slope of each segment?

_____

5 Barb drew a line through the origin and point (2, 3). Jamal drew a line through the origin and point (4, 6). How can you tell that Barb and Jamal drew the same line?

_____

_____

_____

Use the slope formula to determine if the three points lie on a line.

6 $(-3, -2), (-1, 3), (3, 13)$

Do the points lie on the same line? Explain.

_____

7 $(-3, 11), (2, 7), (6, 3)$

Do the points lie on the same line? Explain.

_____

I see! I can think of any two points as the endpoints of a segment.

DISCUSS

Reasoning with Graphs

Do any segments within each of these graphs share an endpoint? Explain.

I get it! I can relate the steepness of a line with the value of its slope.

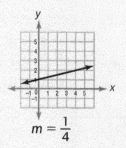

$m = \frac{1}{4}$

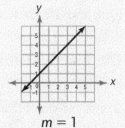

$m = 1$

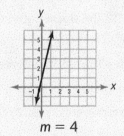

$m = 4$

What do you notice about the slopes as the lines gets steeper?

PROBLEM SOLVING

UNDERWATER PRESSURE

READ

The units of measure for pressure are called atmospheres. The pressure at sea level is 1 atmosphere. At a depth of 20 meters, the pressure is 3 atmospheres. Write an equation, and find the pressure at a depth of 100 meters.

PLAN

• You need to find the number of atmospheres at a depth of _____.

• Use (0, 1) for the pressure at _____.

• Use _____ for the pressure at a depth of 20 meters.

• Use the points to find the _____.

• Use the measure of pressure at _____ as the y-intercept.

• Use $y = mx + b$ and substitute _____ for x.

SOLVE

Write an equation.

The slope, $m = \dfrac{\boxed{3} - \boxed{1}}{\boxed{} - \boxed{}} = \dfrac{\boxed{}}{\boxed{}} = \dfrac{\boxed{}}{\boxed{}}$

The y-intercept is _____. The equation is $y = \dfrac{\boxed{}}{\boxed{}}x + \boxed{}$.

Find the number of atmospheres at a depth of 100 meters: $y = \frac{1}{10}(\underline{}) + 1 = \underline{}$

CHECK

Write an ordered pair for the atmosphere at a depth of 100 meters. (100, $\boxed{}$)

Check that this point and the given two points lie on the same line.

The slope between (0, 1) and (20, 3) is _____.

The slope between (20, 3) and (100, 11) is: $m = \dfrac{\boxed{} - \boxed{}}{\boxed{} - \boxed{}} = \dfrac{\boxed{}}{\boxed{}} = \dfrac{\boxed{}}{\boxed{}}$

The slopes are _____, so the points _____.

At a depth of 100 meters, the pressure is _____ atmospheres.

PRACTICE

Use the problem-solving steps to help you.

1 A computer repair company charges $50 for an appointment. For 2 hours of repair work, it charges a total of $120. What is the total charge for 5 hours of repair work?

> I see! For the company to perform any repair work, a customer is charged for making an appointment. That amount is the y-intercept!

CHECKLIST
- [ ] READ
- [ ] PLAN
- [ ] SOLVE
- [ ] CHECK

2 At dawn, the temperature is 70°F. The temperature falls at the same rate for the rest of the day. In 4 hours, the temperature is 60°F. What is the temperature 6 hours after dawn?

CHECKLIST
- [ ] READ
- [ ] PLAN
- [ ] SOLVE
- [ ] CHECK

3 Jennie works for a cell phone company. She earns $250 per week plus commissions she makes on sales. One week, she had sales of $1000, and her pay was $275. How much would her pay be if she had sales of $2,000?

CHECKLIST
- [ ] READ
- [ ] PLAN
- [ ] SOLVE
- [ ] CHECK

Linear Equations with Rational Coefficients

PLUG IN Interpreting Solutions of Equations

The solution to an **algebraic equation** with one **variable** is any value of the variable that makes both sides equal.

This equation has one solution.

$x + 2 = 5$

$x = 3$

I see! The only number that can be added to 2 to get 5 is 3.

If the **expressions** on both sides of an equation are identical or proportional, the equation has infinitely many solutions.

This equation has infinitely many solutions.

$x + 2 = x + 2 \leftarrow$ always true

$3 + 2 = 3 + 2 \leftarrow x$ could be 3.

$0 + 2 = 0 + 2 \leftarrow x$ could be 0.

I get it! Any value of x makes the equation true.

If the expressions on both sides of an equation can never be equal, the equation has no solution.

This equation has no solutions.

$x + 2 = x - 2 \leftarrow$ never true

$3 + 2 \neq 3 - 2 \leftarrow x \neq 3$

$0 + 2 \neq 0 - 2 \leftarrow x \neq 0$

Right! $2 \neq -2$, so there is no value of x that will make the equation true.

 Words to Know

algebraic equation
a number sentence with at least one variable and an equal sign

variable
a letter or symbol used to stand for one or more numbers

expression
a mathematical phrase containing numbers and/or variables and operations

DISCUSS Emma says that the variable n in an equation always stands for exactly one number. What can you tell Emma about her work?

A Simplify an equation to determine its number of solutions.

 DO Solve for a: $5a = 20$

Fractions are one way to show division.

❶ Identify the inverse operation to isolate the variable.

❷ Use the same operation on both sides to make both sides equal.

❸ Simplify to solve for a.

❹ Interpret the solution.

The inverse of multiplication is _____.

So divide $5a$ by _____ to get a by itself.

$5a \div$ _____ $= 20 \div$ _____

_____ $=$ _____

The equation has _____ solution(s).

> To keep an equation balanced, I have to perform the same operation on both sides of an equation.

B Simplify an equation to determine its number of solutions.

DO Solve for x: $x + 5 - 3 = x + 8$

① Simplify the equation. Subtract 3 from 5.

$$x + 5 - 3 = x + 8$$

② Subtract x from both sides.

$$x + \underline{\hspace{1cm}} = x + 8$$

③ Compare the expressions on both sides of the simplified equation. Write = or ≠.

$$x - \underline{\hspace{1cm}} + 2 = x - \underline{\hspace{1cm}} + 8$$

$$2 \bigcirc 8$$

④ Interpret the solution.

The equation has _____ solution(s), because $2 = 8$ is _____ true.

C Simplify an equation to determine its number of solutions.

DO Solve for n: $n - 4 = n - (8 \div 2)$

$$n - 4 = n - (8 \div 2)$$

① Simplify inside the parentheses.

$$n - 4 = n - \underline{\hspace{1cm}}$$

② Subtract n from both sides.

$$n - \underline{\hspace{1cm}} - 4 = n - \underline{\hspace{1cm}} - 4$$

③ Compare the expressions on both sides of the equation using the = or ≠ symbol.

$$-4 \bigcirc -4$$

④ Interpret the solution.

The equation has _____ solution(s), because the equation $-4 = -4$ is _____ true.

DISCUSS Describe simplified equations that have one solution, infinitely many solutions, or no solution.

PRACTICE

State if each equation has no solution, one solution, or infinitely many solutions.

1 $g + 10 = g - 10$

_____

2 $2 + m = 3$

_____

3 $4b = 4b$

_____

4 $3k = 6$

_____

Solve for x. If there are infinitely many solutions, write *infinitely many solutions*. If there is no solution, write *no solution*.

5 $\frac{x}{3} = 6$

$x =$ _____

6 $x - 4 = x - 5 + 1$

$x =$ _____

7 $x - (8 - 3) = x - 11$

$x =$ _____

8 $x + (3 - 1) = 4$

$x =$ _____

You can apply the **distributive property** to solve some equations. This property describes how to multiply one term by a sum or difference in parentheses. Sometimes, you need to combine **like terms** to solve an equation. To add like terms, add the **coefficients**. To subtract like terms, subtract the coefficients.

Solve the equation for x.

$3(2x + 5) - 4x = 5x$

1. Use the distributive property to multiply each term in the sum $2x + 5$ by 3.

2. Subtract the coefficients in $4x$ and $6x$ to combine like terms.

3. Subtract $2x$ from both sides of the equation to get all the variables on one side.

4. Divide both sides of the equation by 3 to isolate the variable.

$$3(2x + 5) - 4x = 5x$$
$$(3 \cdot 2x) + (3 \cdot 5) - 4x = 5x$$
$$6x + 15 - 4x = 5x$$
$$(6x - 4x) + 15 = 5x$$
$$2x + 15 = 5x$$
$$2x - 2x + 15 = 5x - 2x$$
$$\frac{15}{3} = \frac{3x}{3}$$
$$x = 5$$

> I see! By applying the distributive property, I can then apply operations to isolate the variable.

Words to Know

distributive property	like terms	coefficient
a property that states that the product of a factor and a sum is equal to the sum of the products of the factor and each addend; also applies to the product of a factor and a difference	terms that have the same variable raised to the same exponent	a number that is multiplied by a variable

DISCUSS

Why can only like terms be combined through addition and subtraction? Why is it not possible to combine a variable term and a constant through addition or subtraction, for example?

A Use the distributive property to find the solution(s), if any, for an equation.

 DO

Solve for x: $4(x - 3) = 4x - 3$

1. Apply the distributive property to the left side of the equation.

2. Subtract $4x$ from both sides of the equation.

3. Interpret the solution.

$$4(x - 3) = 4x - 3$$
$$(4 \cdot \underline{\quad}) - (4 \cdot \underline{\quad}) = 4x - 3$$
$$\underline{\quad} - \underline{\quad} = 4x - 3$$
$$4x - \underline{\quad} - 12 = 4x - \underline{\quad} - 3$$
$$\underline{\quad} \neq \underline{\quad}$$

The equation has _____ solution(s), because $-12 = -3$

is _____ true.

B Apply the distributive property and combine like terms to find the solution(s), if any, for an equation.

DO   Solve for k: $3(k + 5) = 4k + 10 - k + 5$

❶ Apply the distributive property.

❷ Combine like terms and perform operations to isolate the variable.

❸ Interpret the solution.

$3(k + 5) = 4k + 10 - k + 5$

$(3 \cdot \underline{\quad}) + (3 \cdot \underline{\quad}) - 4k + 10 - k + 5$

$\underline{\quad\quad} + \underline{\quad\quad} = 4k + 10 - k + 5$

$3k + 15 = 4k - \underline{\quad\quad} + 10 + \underline{\quad\quad}$

$3k + 15 = \underline{\quad\quad} + \underline{\quad\quad}$

The equation has \underline{\quad\quad\quad\quad} solution(s) because $3k + 15 = 3k + 15$ will \underline{\quad\quad\quad} be true.

DISCUSS   Kurt simplifies this equation and says it has no solution. What can you tell Kurt about his work?

$2(x - 7) = 2x - 14$

$2x - 7 = 2x - 14$

$-7 = -14$

PRACTICE

Use the distributive property to solve for x. If there are infinitely many solutions, write *infinitely many solutions*. If there is no solution, write *no solution*.

1 $5(x + 1) = 10$

$x = \underline{\quad\quad\quad}$

2 $8(x - 4) = 8x - 32$

$x = \underline{\quad\quad\quad}$

Combine like terms to solve for n. If there are infinitely many solutions, write *infinitely many solutions*. If there is no solution, write *no solution*.

3 $11n - 4 - 3n = 8n - 5$

$n = \underline{\quad\quad\quad}$

4 $4n + 5 = 8n + 3$

$n = \underline{\quad\quad\quad}$

Apply the distributive property and combine like terms to solve for b.

5 $5(b - 1) + 7 = 6b + 1$

$b = \underline{\quad\quad}$

6 $3(5b + 2) - b = 4(b + 9)$

$b = \underline{\quad\quad}$

READY TO GO

Linear Equations with Rational Coefficients

Some algebraic equations have coefficients that include **rational numbers,** which include fractions, decimals, and negative **integers**.

Solve for x: $\frac{1}{3}(4x - 3) = \frac{2}{3}x - 5 + 2x$

1. Apply the distributive property.

2. Rename the whole number coefficient of a variable term to combine like terms.

3. Isolate the variable.

4. Solve for x.

> I see! I can multiply both sides by the reciprocal of the coefficient. The reciprocal of a number is its multiplicative inverse.

$$\frac{1}{3}(4x - 3) = \frac{2}{3}x - 5 + 2x$$

$$\left(\frac{1}{3} \cdot 4x\right) - \left(\frac{1}{3} \cdot 3\right) = \frac{2}{3}x - 5 + 2x$$

$$\frac{4}{3}x - 1 = \frac{2}{3}x - 5 + 2x$$

$$\frac{4}{3}x - 1 = \frac{2}{3}x + 2x - 5$$

$$\frac{4}{3}x - 1 = \frac{2}{3}x + \frac{6}{3}x - 5$$

$$\frac{4}{3}x - 1 = \frac{8}{3}x - 5$$

$$\frac{4}{3}x - \frac{4}{3}x - 1 = \frac{8}{3}x - \frac{4}{3}x - 5$$

$$-1 = \frac{4}{3}x - 5$$

$$-1 + 5 = \frac{4}{3}x - 5 + 5$$

$$4 = \frac{4}{3}x$$

$$\frac{4}{1} \cdot \frac{3}{4} = \frac{4}{3}x \cdot \frac{3}{4}$$

$$3 = x$$

Words to Know

rational number
a number that can be written as the ratio of two integers

integers
counting numbers (1, 2, 3, ...), their opposites (−1, −2, −3, ...), and zero

DISCUSS How is solving an equation with rational coefficients like solving an equation with whole-number coefficients?

LESSON LINK

PLUG IN	POWER UP	GO!

PLUG IN

You can simplify an equation to determine if it has no solution, one solution, or infinitely many solutions.

$$6x = 2$$
$$\frac{6x}{6} = \frac{2}{6}$$
$$x = \frac{1}{3} \leftarrow \text{one solution}$$

POWER UP

You can use the distributive property and combine like terms to solve equations with whole-number coefficients.

$$2(x - 1) - x = 4$$
$$2x - 2 - x = 4$$
$$x - 2 = 4$$
$$x = 6$$

GO!

> I get it! I can apply the same strategies for solving equations with whole number coefficients to solve equations with rational number coefficients.

WORK TOGETHER

Solve for a:
$1.5(2a + 4) = -6.5a - 3 + 0.5a$

- Apply the distributive property.

- Apply the commutative property.

- Combine like terms.

- Isolate the variable and solve for a.

$a = -1$

$$1.5(2a + 4) = -6.5a - 3 + 0.5a$$
$$(1.5 \cdot 2a) + (1.5 \cdot 4) = -6.5a - 3 + 0.5a$$
$$3a + 6 = -6.5a - 3 + 0.5a$$
$$3a + 6 = -6.5a + 0.5a - 3$$
$$3a + 6 = -6a - 3$$
$$3a - 3a + 6 = -6a - 3a - 3$$
$$6 = -9a - 3$$
$$6 + 3 = -9a - 3 + 3$$
$$9 = -9a$$
$$\frac{9}{-9} = \frac{-9a}{-9}$$
$$-1 = a$$

> **Properties of Multiplication** can be found on p. 215

A Solve an equation with fractional coefficients.

DO

Solve for c: $-\frac{1}{5}c + 2 + c = \frac{1}{5}(10c - 20)$

> I know a variable without a coefficient is the same as I times that variable. So I can rewrite the coefficient 1 as $\frac{5}{5}$.

❶ Apply the distributive property.

❷ Use the commutative property and combine like terms.

❸ Isolate the variable.

❹ Multiply both sides by the reciprocal of the coefficient to solve for c.

$$-\frac{1}{5}c + 2 + c = \frac{1}{5}(10c - 20)$$
$$-\frac{1}{5}c + 2 + c = \left(\frac{1}{5} \cdot \underline{\qquad}\right) - \left(\frac{1}{5} \times \underline{\qquad}\right)$$
$$-\frac{1}{5}c + 2 + c = \underline{\qquad} - \underline{\qquad}$$
$$-\frac{1}{5}c + c + \underline{\qquad} = 2c - 4$$
$$-\frac{1}{5}c + \frac{5}{5}c + \underline{\qquad} = 2c - 4$$
$$\underline{\qquad} + 2 = 2c - \underline{\qquad}$$
$$\frac{4}{5}c - \underline{\qquad} + 2 = \frac{10}{5}c - \underline{\qquad} - 4$$
$$2 = \underline{\qquad} - \underline{\qquad}$$
$$2 + \underline{\qquad} = \frac{6}{5}c - 4 + \underline{\qquad}$$
$$\underline{\qquad} = \underline{\qquad}$$
$$6 \cdot \underline{\qquad} = \frac{6}{5}c \cdot \underline{\qquad}$$
$$\underline{\qquad} = c$$

> I can rewrite 2c in the equivalent form of $\frac{10}{5}c$ to make subtraction easier.

DISCUSS

How do you know when you are finished simplifying an equation with one variable?

PRACTICE

Apply the distributive property to solve for *k*. If there are infinitely many solutions, write *infinitely many solutions*. If there is no solution, write *no solution*.

1 $\frac{1}{3}k - 3 + 1 = \frac{1}{3}(k - 6)$

_____

REMEMBER
Start by applying the distributive property to the right side of the equation.

2 $0.1(10k - 15) = 2$

_____

HINT
Remember to write the solution of an equation by stating the variable and an equal sign. For example, $x = 5$.

Combine like terms to solve for *a*. If there are infinitely many solutions, write *infinitely many solutions*. If there is no solution, write *no solution*.

3 $\frac{3}{4}a + 7 = a - 1$

_____

4 $2.1a + 3 = 2.1a - 2$

_____

Apply the distributive property and combine like terms to solve for *x*.

5 $-4(x + 2) = -3.5x + 2$

_____

6 $\frac{1}{2}(2x - 2) = 5x + 4$

_____

Solve for z. If there are infinitely many solutions, write *infinitely many solutions*. If there is no solution, write *no solution*.

7 $0.5(10z + 20) - 5 = 0.1(50z + 50)$

_____

8 $\frac{3}{2}(6z + 4) + 2z = 2(z - 6)$

_____

9 $\frac{1}{4}(20z + 3) = \frac{3}{4}(8z + 1)$

_____

10 $-4(2.5z + 3) = -8.5z - 15 - 1.5z$

_____

Solve each equation to convert a temperature between the Fahrenheit scale and the Celsius scale.

> I get it! I can solve each of these one-variable equations to find the temperature in a different unit of measurement.

11 When it is 41°F outside, Jana converts the temperature to °C by solving the following equation for x. What is the temperature in °C?

$41 = \frac{9}{5}x + 32$

_____ °Celsius

12 When it is 10°C outside, Yuri converts the temperature to °F by solving the following equation for y. What is the temperature in °F?

$10 = \frac{5}{9}(y - 32)$

_____ °Fahrenheit

> First, I'll simplify the equation. Then, I'll think of values that complete the equation and fit the description.

 DISCUSS   **Make Sense of Problems**

Use reasoning to identify a number that results in the solution described.

Infinitely Many Solutions	No Solution	One Solution
$-\frac{1}{2}(3x - 8) = -\frac{3}{2}x + \underline{\quad}$	$-\frac{1}{2}(3x - 8) = -\frac{3}{2}x + \underline{\quad}$	$-\frac{1}{2}(3x - 8) = \underline{\quad}x + 4$

PROBLEM SOLVING

ALL IS FARE

READ

The fare for a taxi ride is $2.50 for the first mile and $1.50 for each additional mile. Madeline pays $17.50 for a taxi ride. Use the equation to find how many miles, m, she traveled.

$2.50 + 1.50(m − 1) = 17.50$

PLAN

• Find the _____ Madeline traveled in the taxi.

• To find the answer, solve the given equation for _____.

SOLVE

Apply the distributive property and combine like terms.

$2.50 + 1.50(m − 1) = 17.50$

_____2.50_____ + _____ − _____ = _____

_____1.00_____ + _____ = _____

Isolate the variable and solve for m.

_____ − _____ + _____ = _____ − _____

_____ = _____

$$\frac{\boxed{}}{\boxed{}} = \frac{\boxed{}}{\boxed{}}$$

$m =$ _____

I see! If my answer is correct, I can substitute it for m in the original equation and produce a true statement.

CHECK

Substitute the value of m into the original equation. Then solve.

Write the original equation.

_____ + _____ (_____ − _____) = _____

Replace the variable, m, with the solution and simplify.

_____ + _____ (_____ − _____) = _____

_____ + _____ (_____) = _____

_____ + _____ = _____

_____ = _____

The statement is _____.

Madeline traveled _____ miles.

PRACTICE

Use the problem-solving steps to help you.

1 Gina's cell phone plan costs $49.95 per month plus $0.15 for each minute of calls over the first 200 minutes. Her bill this month was $64.95. Use the equation below to find how many minutes, m, of phone calls she made.

$49.95 + 0.15(m - 200) = \$64.95$

---

2 A rectangular sandbox has a perimeter of 18 feet. The width of the sandbox is w feet and the length is $\frac{4}{3}w + 2$ feet. Use the equation below to find the length and the width of the sandbox.

$2(\frac{4}{3}w + 2) + 2w = 18$

I get it! I solve the equation for w to find the width, and then substitute the solution into $\frac{4}{3}w + 2$ to find the length.

---

3 Matt is training for a race. In the past 3 weeks, he has run a total of $20\frac{1}{2}$ miles. He ran m miles the first week, $m + 2$ miles the second week, and $\frac{1}{2}(m + 2)$ miles the third week. Solve the equation below to find how many miles he ran each week.

$m + (m + 2) + \frac{1}{2}(m + 2) = 20\frac{1}{2}$

Week 1 = m

Week 2 = $m + 2$

Week 3 = $\frac{1}{2}(m + 2)$

I can solve the main equation for m to find how far he ran the first week. Then I can substitute the value of m into the weekly equations to find how far he ran during weeks 2 and 3.

Linear Equations in Two Variables

PLUG IN Solving Linear Systems Graphically

The graph of a linear equation with two **variables** x and y shows all pairs of x and y that make the equation true.

$$y = 3x - 2$$

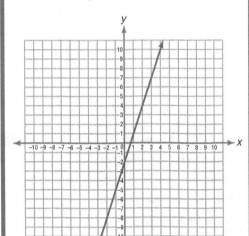

A solution to a **system of equations** is a pair of x and y values that makes the equations true.

System of equations:

Equation 1:
$$y = 3x - 2$$

Equation 2:
$$y = 2x + 1$$

The **intersection** of lines on a graph is represented by a coordinate pair (x, y). This point is a solution to the system of equations.

Equation 1: $y = 3x - 2$

Equation 2: $y = 2x + 1$

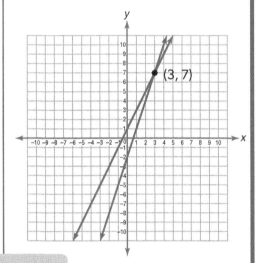

(3, 7)

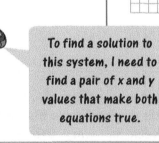

If an equation is true, the left side of the equation equals the right side.

To find a solution to this system, I need to find a pair of x and y values that make both equations true.

The point (3, 7) is the intersection of both lines. So the solution to the system is (3, 7).

Words to Know

variable
a letter or symbol used to stand for one or more numbers

system of equations
two or more equations with the same variables

intersection
the point or points where graphs of equations meet

DISCUSS

Sam graphs two linear equations and sees the lines are parallel. He knows this means the lines never cross. If the lines never cross, does this system of equations have a solution?

A You can find the solution to a system of linear equations by finding their point of intersection.

What is the solution to the system $y = -x - 1$ and $y = 3x + 11$?

1 Find several ordered pairs for each equation.

2 Graph the system of equations.

3 Check the solution.

$y = -x - 1$

x	y
−1	
0	
1	
2	

$y = 3x + 11$

x	y
−1	
0	
1	
−5	

The graphs intersect at _____.

$y = -x - 1$

_____ = −(_____) − 1

_____ = _____ − 1

_____ = _____

$y = 3x + 11$

_____ = 3(_____) + 11

_____ = _____ + 11

_____ = _____

The ordered pair _____ satisfies both equations, so the solution is correct.

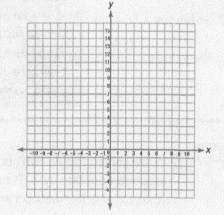

 DISCUSS Julie graphs a system of linear equations twice. The first time, she draws it on a coordinate grid whose scale is from −10 to 10 for the x and y axes. The second time, she draws it on a coordinate grid whose scale is from −5 to 5 for the x and y axes. She sees the lines intersect on the first graph but not on the second graph. Does this system of equations have a solution? Explain.

PRACTICE

Find the solution to the system of linear equations by graphing.

1 $y = -5x - 10$

$y = -x + 2$

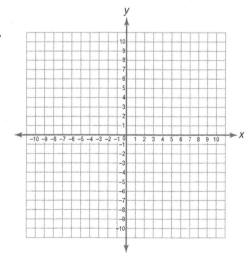

The solution is _____.

Solve Linear Systems Algebraically

You can solve a system of equations algebraically.

① **Line up the equations and compare coefficients.** Neither the x-coefficients nor the y-coefficients are the same or opposite.

② **Multiply both sides of one or both equations by a factor.** Write an equivalent equation so that the coefficients of one variable in the system are the same or opposite.

③ **Add the equations.** Because the y-coefficients are opposites, you can eliminate the y terms through addition.

④ **Solve for x.**

⑤ **Solve for y.** Use the value for x to find the value of y.

The solution is (3, 7).

> I see! I can eliminate one variable through addition or subtraction. Then I can solve for the other variable.

Solve the system $-3x + y = -2$ and $-2x + y = 1$.

$$-3x + y = -2$$
$$-2x + y = 1$$

$$-1(-3x + y) = -1(-2)$$
$$-2x + y = 1$$

$$\begin{array}{r} 3x - y = 2 \\ + \quad -2x + y = 1 \\ \hline x + 0y = 3 \end{array}$$

$$x = 3$$

$$-3(3) + y = -2$$
$$-9 + y = -2$$
$$-9 + y + 9 = -2 + 9$$
$$y = 7$$

DISCUSS Cora solved the system above by multiplying the first equation by 2 and multiplying the second equation by 3. Then she subtracted the second equation from the first equation. Explain why her method works.

A You can solve a system of equations algebraically.

DO

Solve the system $2x + y = 9$ and $3x - y = 16$.

① Line up the equations.

② Add the equations.

③ Solve for x.

④ Solve for y. Use the value for x to find the value of y.

⑤ Write the solution.

$$\begin{array}{r} 2x + y = 9 \\ + \quad 3x - y = 16 \\ \hline \underline{\quad}x + 0y = \underline{\quad}, \text{ so } x = \underline{\quad} \end{array}$$

$$2(\underline{\quad}) + y = 9$$
$$\underline{\quad} + y = 9$$
$$\underline{\quad} + y - \underline{\quad} = 9 - \underline{\quad}$$
$$y = \underline{\quad}$$

> I remember! The term 0y is equal to 0.

The solution to the system is _____.

B You can solve a system of linear equations algebraically.

DO Solve the system $x - 2y = -9$ and $x + 3y = 16$.

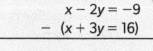

I see! The x-coefficients are already the same, so I didn't need to multiply either equation by a factor.

1. Line up the equations.
2. Subtract the equations.
3. Solve for y.
4. Solve for x. Use the value for y to find the value of x.
5. Write the solution.

$$x - 2y = -9$$
$$-\ (x + 3y = 16)$$
$$\underline{\hspace{1cm}}x\ |\ \underline{\hspace{1cm}}y = \underline{\hspace{1cm}}, \text{ so } y = \underline{\hspace{1cm}}$$
$$x - 2(\underline{\hspace{1cm}}) = -9$$
$$x - \underline{\hspace{1cm}} = -9$$
$$x - \underline{\hspace{1cm}} + \underline{\hspace{1cm}} = -9 + \underline{\hspace{1cm}}$$
$$x = \underline{\hspace{1cm}}$$

The solution to the system is _____.

DISCUSS Edward says he checks the solution he found on a graph by substituting it into both equations of the system. How will he know if his answer is right?

PRACTICE

Solve each system of equations algebraically.

1 $2x - y = 9$
$3x + 4y = -14$

2 $4x - 3y = 25$
$-3x + 8y = 10$

3 $3x - 4y = 17$
$-2x + y = -8$

4 $x - 3y = 7$
$3x + 5y = -7$

5 $x - 3y = -5$
$3x + 4y = 11$

6 $5x - 4y = 24$
$-7x - 2y = 12$

7 $-3x - 7y = -18$
$-5x - 3y = -4$

8 $7x - 9y = 3$
$8x - 7y = 10$

Linear Equations in Two Variables

You can represent many situations using equations.

Cameron compares the costs of two cell phone text messaging plans. Plan 1 costs $5.00 a month, plus $0.05 for each text message sent. Plan 2 costs $0.00 a month, plus $0.10 for each text message sent.

Plan 1: $y = 5 + 0.05x$

Plan 2: $y = 0.10x$

Graphing the two equations shows where they intersect. The intersection is the coordinate pair (x, y) that is a solution to the system of equations.

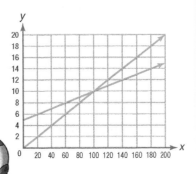

You can also solve the system algebraically. Since each equation equals y, the other sides of those equations are equal to each other.

$$y = 5 + 0.05x$$

$$y = 0.10x$$

$$5 + 0.05x = 0.10x$$

$$5 = 0.05x$$

$$x = 100$$

$$y = 0.10(100)$$

$$y = 10$$

On both plans, if he sends 100 text messages, the cost is the same: $10.

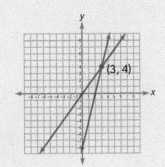

> I see. In each equation, x is the number of text messages sent, and y is the total cost in dollars.

> On the graph, the x-axis is number of text messages sent, and the y-axis is the cost in dollars.

> I see! Since $y = 0.10x$, I can substitute $0.10x$ for y in the other equation. Then the only variable left to solve for is x.

 DISCUSS What is an advantage of using algebra instead of a graph to solve a system of equations?

LESSON LINK

PLUG IN

You can solve a system of linear equations using a graph.

$$y = x$$

$$y = 4x - 8$$

(3, 4)

POWER UP

You can solve a system of linear equations using algebra.

$$y = x + 3$$
$$y = -x + 5$$
$$2y = 8$$
$$y = 4$$

So, $x = 1$.

The solution to the system is (1, 4).

GO!

> I get it! I can solve systems of equations related to real-world situations using graphs or algebra.

WORK TOGETHER

You can graph a system of equations that model a situation to find a solution.

- Graph the first equation.
- Graph the second equation on the same coordinate grid.
- Identify the coordinates of a point of intersection.
- Make sense of the answer.

Two classes collect cans to recycle. One teacher brings in 15 cans and asks each of his students to bring in 2 more cans. Another teacher brings in 5 cans and asks each of her students to bring in 3 more cans. In the system of equations, y is the number of cans collected in each class, and x is the number of students in each class.

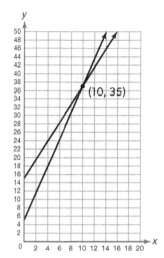

$$y = 15 + 2x$$

$$y = 5 + 3x$$

The intersection is (10, 35). This means if there are 10 students in each class, then each class will collect 35 cans.

A You can solve a system of linear equations that represent real-life situations.

DO

A ticket for a fair is $2 for children and $4 for adults. On a certain day, 1,000 people attended the fair, and $2,600 is collected. How many children and how many adults attended on that day?

> I see! I have a lot of choices when I solve. I could have multiplied both sides of the first equation by 2 so that the coefficients of x were the same, or −2 so they were opposites.

1️⃣ Write a system of equations to represent the situation.
Let x represent the number of children.
Let y represent the number of adults.

$x + y = \boxed{}$

$2x + 4y = \boxed{}$

$4(x + y) = 4(1,000)$, so $4x + 4y = \boxed{}$

2️⃣ Multiply one equation so the y coefficients match.

3️⃣ Subtract the equations.

$$\begin{aligned} 4x + 4y &= 4,000 \\ -(2x + 4y &= 2,600) \\ \hline 2x &= \boxed{} \end{aligned}$$, so $x = \boxed{}$

4️⃣ Solve for x.

5️⃣ Substitute the value of x into the first equation to find y.

$700 + y = 1,000$

$700 + y - 700 = 1,000 - \boxed{}$, so $y = \boxed{}$

6️⃣ Make sense of the answer.

The point of intersection is (700, 300). So _____ children and _____ adults attended that day.

DISCUSS

Jasper solved a system of equations and found a value for x. He wasn't sure which equation he should substitute this value into to find y. What would you tell Jasper?

PRACTICE

Solve.

1 A test has 20 questions worth a total of 100 points. The test has some true/false questions worth 3 points each. The rest are multiple-choice questions worth 11 points each. How many questions of each type are on the test?

Let x represent the number of true/false questions.

Let y represent the number of multiple-choice questions.

2 Catalina buys food and medicine for the dogs at a pet store. She spends 4 times as much on food as she spends on medicine. She spends a total of $400. How much did Catalina spend on food and on medicine?

Let x represent the amount spent on food.

Let y represent the amount spent on medication.

3 Irene has a collection of 32 dolls that have either blue eyes or green eyes. She has 14 more green-eyed dolls than blue-eyed dolls. How many dolls of each type does Irene have?

Let x represent the number of green-eyed dolls.

Let y represent the number of blue-eyed dolls.

Solve.

4 Quinn and Derek bought office supplies together. Quinn bought 10 packs of paper and 12 boxes of pens for a total cost of $33. Derek bought 15 packs of paper and 7 boxes of pens for a total of $27.50. How much was one pack of paper? How much was one box of pens?

5 Diego ran a lemonade stand where he sold small cups of lemonade for $1 and large cups for $3.00. Diego sold a total of 75 cups of lemonade. If he collected a total of $125, how many cups of each size did Diego sell?

Solve.

6 Everyone at a park was either hiking or riding a bike. There were 24 more hikers than bike riders. If there were a total of 100 people at the park, how many were hiking? _____

I know! I'll start by defining the variables. Then I can write equations using the given information.

7 Linda downloaded 4 movies and 3 TV shows for a total cost of $13. James downloaded 6 movies and 2 TV shows for a total of $17. How much did one movie download cost? _____

DISCUSS

Model with Mathematics

Jill's school can rent buses from one of two companies. The first company charges $500, plus $5 per student. The second company charges $800, plus $2 per student. Jill writes the following equations, where the cost is y and x is the number of students:

Company 1: $y = \$500 + \$5x$

Company 2: $y = \$800 + \$2x$

Jill wants to figure out the number of students for which both companies would charge the same amount. She sees y in both equations and says that both companies always charge the same amount. How would you explain her mistake to her?

I can see Jill's equations are correct. So her mistake must be in her reasoning.

PROBLEM SOLVING

ICE CREAM FUND-RAISER

READ

Mrs. Foster's students hold an ice cream fund-raiser for charity. The cost for renting an ice cream truck is $300. The cost of the ice cream they sell is $0.50 per scoop. The students sell the ice cream for $2.00 per scoop. How many scoops of ice cream do Mrs. Foster's students need to sell so that their sales equal their costs?

PLAN

• What is the problem asking you to do?

Find how many _____ must be sold for sales to equal costs.

• How can you solve this problem?

Write a system of equations.

SOLVE

Solve the system algebraically.

$$y = 300 + 0.5x$$

$$y = 2x$$

Substitute $2x$ for y in the first equation. Solve for x.

$2x = 300 + 0.5x$

$2x - 0.5x = 300 + 0.5x -$ ☐

$1.5x = 300$, so $x = 300 \div 1.5 =$ ☐

Substitute 200 for x to find y.

$y = 2(200) =$ ☐

I see! In both equations, y is the amount of money in dollars. In the first equation, y is the cost. In the second equation, y is the sales.

CHECK

Substitute the answers in each equation to check.

$y = 300 + 0.5x$ $y = 2x$

☐ $= 300 + 0.5($ ☐ $)$ ☐ $= 2($ ☐ $)$

☐ $= 300 +$ ☐   ☐ $=$ ☐

☐ $=$ ☐

Both statements are true, so the answers check.

Mrs. Foster's students must sell _____ scoops of ice cream so that their total sales equal their costs, which are _____.

PRACTICE

Use the problem-solving steps to help you.

1 Charlie and Mara are babysitters. Charlie charges $10 plus $6 per hour. Mara charges $8 per hour. For what number of hours will Charlie and Mara charge the same amount? How much would they charge for that number of hours?

CHECKLIST
- [ ] READ
- [ ] PLAN
- [ ] SOLVE
- [ ] CHECK

2 Oscar is offered jobs at two different dog-walking companies. At Company 1, he would earn $50 a day, plus $6 for each dog walked. At Company 2, he would earn $20 a day, plus $9 for each dog walked. How many dogs would Oscar have to walk to earn the same amount at both companies in a day? How much would he earn for walking that number of dogs?

CHECKLIST
- [ ] READ
- [ ] PLAN
- [ ] SOLVE
- [ ] CHECK

3 Mrs. Keegan will rent one of two theaters for the school play. The first theater will cost $600, and tickets can be sold for $4 each. The second theater will cost $350, and the tickets can be sold for $3 each. How many tickets would the class need to sell for the money earned at each theater to be equal?

CHECKLIST
- [ ] READ
- [ ] PLAN
- [ ] SOLVE
- [ ] CHECK

I see! I'll assign x as the number of tickets sold and y as the amount earned. So I'll write each equation as "the amount earned is equal to the ticket price times the number of tickets sold, less the cost of the theater."

Modeling Relationships with Functions

PLUG IN Understanding Functions

In this **function** table, the x-values are the input values, and the y-values are the output values.

x	1	4	7	5	2	8	9
y	2	5	0	5	6	1	3

A **linear function** is a function represented by a line. A linear function has a constant slope.

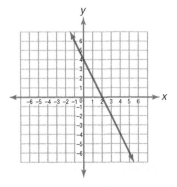

$$y = -2x + 4$$

A **nonlinear function** is a function whose graph is not a line.

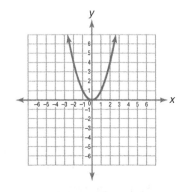

$$y = x^2$$

I see! This table shows a function because each x-value has one, and only one, y-value.

This is a function because there is exactly one y-value for each x-value. And it's linear because it looks like a line!

A function that has an exponent is nonlinear. A nonlinear function does not have a constant slope.

Words to Know

function
a rule that assigns exactly one output value to each input value

linear function
a function whose graph is a straight line

nonlinear function
a function whose graph is not a straight line

DISCUSS
Wade says that $y = x^2 + 2$ is a linear function. What would you say to Wade about his statement?

A You can determine if a function is linear by its graph.

DO
Identify whether each graph shows a linear or nonlinear function.

1 Look at the graph of the function.

2 Determine whether the graph has a constant slope.

3 Tell if the functions are linear or nonlinear.

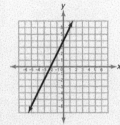

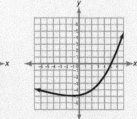

Slope is constant.

It is a _____ function.

Slope is not constant.

It is a _____ function.

I'll sketch a curve or line through each set of points to see if either graph is linear.

B You can determine if a function is linear by values in a table.

Identify whether each table shows a linear or nonlinear function.

1. Plot the points and sketch a line.

2. Determine whether the graph has a constant slope.

3. Tell if the functions are linear or nonlinear.

x	4	3	1	0	1	2
y	5	2	−6	−7	4	−3

x	−4	−2	0	2	4	6
y	−7	−4	−1	2	5	8

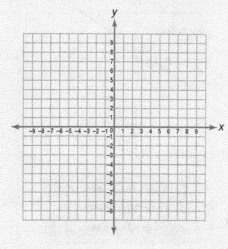

This graph _____ a constant slope.

It is a _____ function.

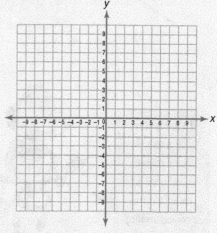

This graph _____ a constant slope.

It is a _____ function.

 DISCUSS Marge asks if there can be a line that is not a linear function. What would you tell her?

PRACTICE

Determine whether each function is *linear* or *nonlinear*.

1

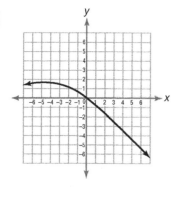

_____

2

x	−2	−1	0	1	2
y	3	1	0	1	3

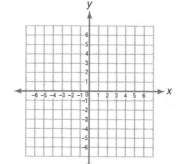

_____

3 $y = 3x - 1$

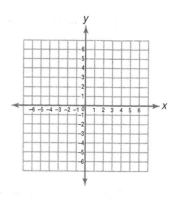

_____

Graphing the Equation $y = mx + b$

A linear function can be written as the equation $y = mx + b$.

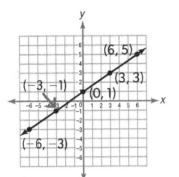

$$y = \frac{2}{3}x + 1$$

To find points on a line, I can select x-values and calculate the corresponding y-values.

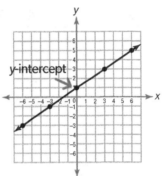

The b in the equation is the **y-intercept**. This is the y-coordinate of the point where the line crosses the y-axis on a graph.

The y-intercept is 1.

I can use the y-intercept as a starting point when I graph a line.

The m in the equation is the **slope** of the line. The value of m tells you the steepness and direction of the line.

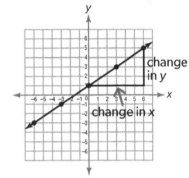

$$m = \frac{\text{change in } y}{\text{change in } x} = \frac{2}{3}$$

I see! If the steepness of a line is constant, then its slope also has a constant value.

Words to Know

y-intercept
the y-coordinate of the point at which a line crosses the y-axis

slope
a ratio of the change in y-coordinates (rise) of a graph to the change in corresponding x-coordinates (run); the symbol for slope is m

DISCUSS   Belinda has plotted one point of a linear function. She asks how she can use the slope to graph the rest of the line. How would you explain it to her?

A You can use the y-intercept and slope to graph a line.

DO   Graph the line $y = \frac{4}{5}x - 3$
using the slope and y-intercept.

❶ Identify and plot the y-intercept.

❷ Use the slope to plot another point.

❸ Draw a line through the points.

The y-intercept is _____.

Find another point 4 units up and 5 units right.

The coordinate pair is (_____, _____).

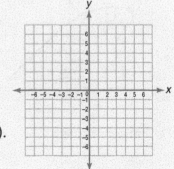

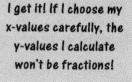

I get it! If I choose my x-values carefully, the y-values I calculate won't be fractions!

B You can graph a line using two points.

DO

Graph the line $y = -\frac{3}{2}x + 1$ by plotting two points.

1 Choose multiples of the denominator of the slope for x-values.

2 Substitute the x-values and compute the y-values.

3 Plot the points and graph the line.

Choose $x = -4$ and $x = 4$.

$y = -\frac{3}{2}(\underline{\hspace{1cm}}) + 1$

$= \underline{\hspace{1cm}} + 1 = \underline{\hspace{1cm}}$

First point: (\underline{\hspace{1cm}}, \underline{\hspace{1cm}})

$y = -\frac{3}{2}(\underline{\hspace{1cm}}) + 1$

$= \underline{\hspace{1cm}} + 1 = \underline{\hspace{1cm}}$

Second point: (\underline{\hspace{1cm}}, \underline{\hspace{1cm}})

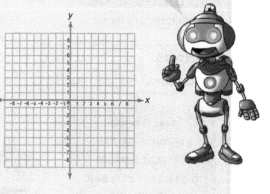

DISCUSS

Tam drew this graph for the equation $y = \frac{2}{3}x + 4$. He says he chose -3 and 3 for x-values.

What would you tell Tam about his mistake in making the graph? How might he have known his graph was incorrect?

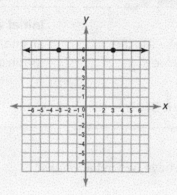

PRACTICE

Graph the line using the slope and y-intercept.

1 $y = -\frac{1}{2}x - 1$

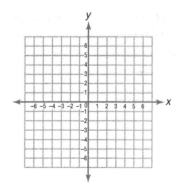

Graph the line using two points.

2 $y = \frac{1}{3}x - 4$

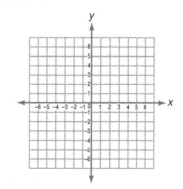

77

Modeling Relationships with Functions

A generator has a 50-gallon tank full of gasoline. It runs at the rate of 5 gallons per hour.

Hours	0	1	2	3
Gallons	50	45	40	35

I see! When the generator runs for 1 hour, it uses up 5 gallons of gas, so it has 45 gallons left.

The **rate of change** of the amount of gasoline remaining is constant: −5 gallons per hour. A constant rate of change is the slope of a linear function.

$$m = -\frac{5 \text{ gallons}}{1 \text{ hour}}$$

The slope is negative because the amount of gasoline decreases as the number of hours increases.

The **initial value**, or starting amount, of gasoline is 50 gallons. So 50 is the y-intercept of a linear function.

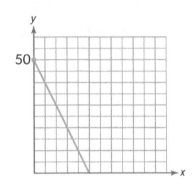

I get it! The initial value is the amount of gasoline left when the generator has run for 0 hours.

 Words to Know

rate of change
the ratio of the change in y-values to the corresponding change in x-values

$$y = 3x + 8$$
The rate of change is 3.

initial value
an interpretation of the y-intercept of the graph of an equation in a real world situation

$$y = 3x + 8$$
The initial value is 8.

DISCUSS Can a linear function have two initial values?

LESSON LINK

PLUG IN
You know a function assigns one output to each input.

x	0	3	5	6	9
y	2	5	3	2	1

POWER UP
You know a linear function has a slope and y-intercept.

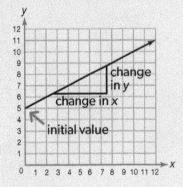

GO!
I get it! I can apply what I know about linear functions to real-world situations, where the slope is the rate of change and the y-intercept is the initial value.

> I know I can model this situation with a linear function because the amount saved was constant. That means the rate of change is constant.

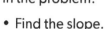
WORK TOGETHER

Find the rate of change and initial value from the data pairs in the problem.

- Find the slope.

- Use the slope to write the equation of the line.

- Substitute a data pair to find the y-intercept.

- Make sense of your answer.

The rate of change is $9 per week. The initial value is $7.

After 2 weeks, Jane had saved $25. After 9 weeks, she had saved $88. If the amount she saved each week was constant, how much did she start with and how much did she save each week? Use the number of weeks for x-values and the amount saved for y values.

The amount she saves is increasing, so the rate of change is positive. For a linear function, the rate of change is the slope.

$$m = \frac{\text{change in } y}{\text{change in } x} = \frac{88 - 25}{9 - 2} = \frac{63}{7} = 9$$

The equation of a linear function that models this situation is $y = 9x + b$.

To find b in $y = 9x + b$, select either data pair. Substitute the values for x and y, and solve for b.

$$25 = 9 \times 2 + b$$

$$25 = 18 + b$$

$$7 = b$$

The equation of the line is $y = 9x + 7$.

A You can find the rate of change and initial value from data pairs.

DO

The table shows the number of forms, y, that are on a clerk's desk x minutes after the starting time. If the number of forms changes at a constant rate, find the rate of change and the initial value.

Time	20	60
Forms	70	150

1 Find the slope.

$$m = \frac{\text{change in } y}{\text{change in } x} = \frac{\boxed{} - \boxed{} = \boxed{}}{\boxed{} - \boxed{} = \boxed{}} = \boxed{}$$

2 Write the equation of a line with the slope.

$$y = \underline{\hspace{1cm}} x + b$$

3 Substitute a data pair to find the y-intercept.

$$\underline{\hspace{1cm}} = \underline{\hspace{1cm}} (\underline{\hspace{1cm}}) + b$$

$$\underline{\hspace{1cm}} = \underline{\hspace{1cm}} + b$$

4 Write the equation of a line with the slope and y-intercept.

$$\underline{\hspace{1cm}} = b$$

$$y = \underline{\hspace{2cm}}$$

The rate of change is \underline{\hspace{1cm}} forms per minute.

The initial value is \underline{\hspace{1cm}} forms.

DISCUSS

How would you know the initial value of a situation is 0 by looking at the linear function that models a situation?

PRACTICE

Graph the line using the slope and y-intercept.

1 $y = \frac{4}{3}x + 1$

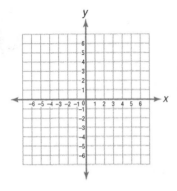

Graph the line using two points.

2 $y = -\frac{3}{5}x + 2$

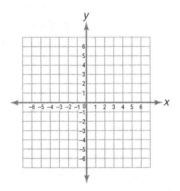

Each situation can be modeled by a linear function. Find the rate of change and initial value.

3 A feather falls from a 105-foot cliff at a rate of 15 feet per minute.

> **REMEMBER**
> Make sure your rate of change has a sign to match its increasing or decreasing value.

rate of change: _____

initial value: _____

4 The amount of water in a new cooler is 6 gallons, and it is used at 0.75 gallons per second.

rate of change: _____

initial value: _____

5 A car salesperson earns $10,000 a year plus $2,000 for each car sold.

rate of change: _____

initial value: _____

6 A submarine dives from sea level at 15 meters each second.

> **HINT**
> You can think of sea level as 0 meters.

rate of change: _____

initial value: _____

7 Two years after a car is purchased, it is worth $24,000. Five years after it is purchased, it is worth $15,000.

rate of change: _____

initial value: _____

8 Sari continued reading a book she had started last week. The table shows her page number based on the numbers of minutes after she started reading today.

Minutes	12	57
Page number	132	147

rate of change: _____

initial value: _____

Find the rate of change and initial value.

9 Ted earns $600 for a 40-hour work week. He earns $450 for a short 30-hour week.

rate of change: _____

initial value: _____

10 The table shows the number of birds flying at different altitudes in the park.

Altitude (feet)	20	40
Number of birds	80	60

rate of change: _____

initial value: _____

Write the equation for the linear function from the indicated problem.

11 A stock value decreases from $95 at the rate of $1 per hour.

_____

12 Charlene pays $50 for internet access and $3 for each movie she downloads.

_____

I'll find the rate of change and the initial value first. Then I'll write $y = mx + b$ using these values.

DISCUSS

Model with Mathematics

Shirley and Mark tried to find the slope between the points (4, 8) and (7, 2). They each computed the change in y and the change in x as shown in the table.

I'll start by writing the formula for slope. Then I'll try the coordinate pairs in the formula in both orders.

Shirley's work	$8 - 2 = 6$	$4 - 7 = -3$
Mark's work	$2 - 8 = -6$	$7 - 4 = 3$

They saw that the order of the values in their calculations were different. When they each calculated the slope with their values, they both found the correct answer, -2. How did this happen?

PROBLEM SOLVING

A MODEL TRAIN MODEL

READ

A model train set with a 50-inch track and train cars costs $65. A model train set with a 200-inch track and the same cars costs $140. If the cost can be modeled by a linear function, find the cost of the train cars and the cost of one inch of the track.

PLAN

• Find a linear function that models the situation.

• Find the _____, which is the initial value,

and the _____, which is the rate of change.

• Use two ordered pairs: (_____, _____) and (_____, _____).

> I see! The cost of the cars is the same for each set. That means that's the initial value of the equation!

SOLVE

Find the slope as a decimal.

$$m = \frac{\text{change in } y}{\text{change in } x} = \frac{\boxed{140} - \boxed{}}{\boxed{200} - \boxed{}} = \frac{\boxed{}}{\boxed{}} = \frac{\boxed{}}{\boxed{}} = \boxed{}$$

$y = $ _____$x + b$

Substitute an ordered pair into the equation to find the y-intercept.

_____ = _____ (_____) + b

_____ = _____ + b

_____ = b

> I can choose either ordered pair to find b. I'll get the same answer either way.

The slope of the line is _____, and the y-intercept is _____.

The equation of the line is _____.

CHECK

To check the answer, substitute the other coordinate pair in the equation.

$y = $ _____$x + $ _____

_____ = _____(_____) + _____

_____ = _____ + _____

_____ = _____

The train cars cost _____ and the track is _____.

PRACTICE

Use the problem-solving steps to help you.

1 After saving newspapers for a project for 3 weeks, Jon had a stack that was 2 feet high. After 6 weeks, the stack was 4 feet high. How high was the stack when Jon started saving the papers? How much higher does the stack get each week?

CHECKLIST
- [ ] READ
- [ ] PLAN
- [ ] SOLVE
- [ ] CHECK

2 Lionel walks home from school. After walking 5 minutes, he is 4,000 feet from home, and after walking 15 minutes he is 2,000 feet from home. How many feet per minute does Lionel walk? How far is his school from his home? How far will he be from home after walking 20 minutes?

I see! After I find the equation, I can substitute a value for time to find how far he is from home at that time.

CHECKLIST
- [ ] READ
- [ ] PLAN
- [ ] SOLVE
- [ ] CHECK

3 After handing out flyers for 2 hours, Larry had 400 flyers left. After 10 hours, he had handed out all of the flyers. How many flyers did Larry start with, and how many did he give out each hour?

CHECKLIST
- [ ] READ
- [ ] PLAN
- [ ] SOLVE
- [ ] CHECK

Comparing Functions

PLUG IN
Describing Functional Relationships from Graphs

Mason made this graph to show the amount of money he makes selling T-shirts.

Describe this functional relationship.

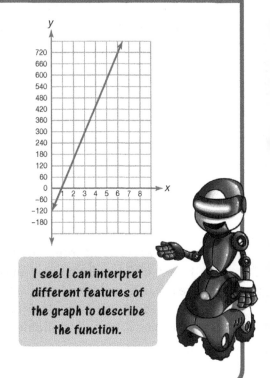

1 **Identify what the *x*- and *y*-coordinates represent.**
In this situation, the *x*-coordinates represent time (in months), and the *y*-coordinates represent money earned (in dollars).

2 **Interpret the *x*-intercept and *y*-intercept.**
The function begins at (0, −120). That means that Mason spent $120 to start selling T-shirts. The function crosses the *x*-axis at 1. That means that Mason made as much as he spent after 1 month of selling T-shirts.

3 **Determine if the function is linear or nonlinear.**
The slope is constant, so the function is linear.

> I see! I can interpret different features of the graph to describe the function.

4 **Interpret the slope.** The function passes through points (1, 0) and (3, 300). Its rate of change is $\frac{300 - 0}{3 - 1} = 150$.
Mason earned $150 each month.

DISCUSS Why would a graph representing the amount of money made over time only include the first quadrant?

A You can use the graph to describe this functional relationship. Include what the *x*-and *y*-coordinates and intercepts represent. Determine what the slope represents.

Susan made a graph to show the amount of money she saved each month.

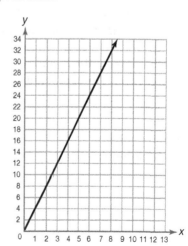

1 Identify what the *x* and *y*-coordinates represent.

The *x*-coordinates represent _____ .

2 Interpret the *x*-intercept and *y*-intercept.

The *y*-coordinates represent _____ .

3 Determine if the function is linear or nonlinear.

The graph has no *x*-intercept. The *y*-intercept is at the point _____ .

4 Interpret the slope of each linear segment.

That means that Susan started with _____ .

The function is made up of two different _____ segments.

Susan saved _____ each month for the first _____ months.

Susan saved _____ each month for the next _____ months .

DISCUSS What do you know about the rate of change of a graph with multiple linear segments?

PRACTICE

Use the graph to describe this functional relationship. Include what the *x*- and *y*-coordinates and intercept represent. Determine if the graph is linear or nonlinear and what the slope of each linear segment represents.

1 This graph represents the relationship between the side length of a square and the perimeter of the square.

_____

_____

_____

_____

_____

Sketching Graphs Using Verbal Descriptions

Lesley is training for a walkathon. She calculated her walking rate is 4 miles an hour.

Sketch a graph that represents this functional relationship.

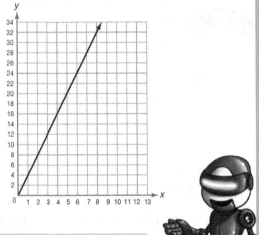

1 **Define what the x- and y-coordinates represent.** In this situation, the x-coordinates represent time (in hours), and the y-coordinates represent distance (in miles).

2 **Determine the initial value.** When x = 0, the distance is 0. The initial value is plotted as (0, 0).

3 **Determine if the function is linear.** The rate of change is constant: 4 miles an hour. So the function is linear.

4 **Determine the slope.** For each hour Lesley walks, she travels a distance of 4 miles. The slope is $\frac{4}{1}$ or 4.

Sketch a graph of a line that passes through (0, 0) with a slope of 4.

> I get it! I can use the initial value and the slope to sketch the graph.

DISCUSS Lesley's friend Patrick trains with her. He walks 4 miles an hour for the first four hours. Then he starts walking 3 miles an hour. How would his graph be different from Lesley's graph?

> I see! I can graph a situation that has more than one linear segment.

A You can sketch a graph based on a verbal description.

DO

Marco starts to fill an empty 20 liter aquarium with water. The amount of water in the aquarium increases by 1 liter per minute. Sketch a graph that represents this functional relationship.

1 Define what the x- and y-coordinates represent.

2 Determine the initial value.

3 If the function is linear, determine the slope.

The x-coordinate represents the

_____.

The y-coordinate represents the _____ of water.

The aquarium starts empty, so at time 0, it holds 0 liters.

The initial value is _____.

The slope is _____.

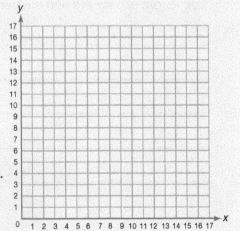

> I see! The graph has a different rate after the first 8 hours. So I'll need two linear segments!

B You can sketch a graph based on a verbal description.

DO

The temperature decreased by 3 degrees Fahrenheit each hour. Then, after 8 hours, the temperature stayed the same for the rest of the day. If the temperature started at 45°F, sketch a graph that represents this functional relationship.

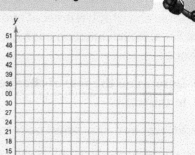

1 Define what the x- and y-coordinates represent.

The x-coordinate represents the time in minutes.

2 Determine the initial value.

The y-coordinate represents the temperature in °F.

3 Determine the slope for each linear segment.

The initial value is 45°F. So the y-intercept is _____.

For the first segment, the slope is _____.

After 8 hours, the temperature stays the same.

For the next segment, the slope is _____.

DISCUSS

How will the values in a table of coordinate pairs for a linear function show that the slope of your graph will be positive or negative?

PRACTICE

Sketch a graph that represents each functional relationship.

1 Ray starts a savings account with $30. He deposits $30 each month for six months. Then he doesn't deposit any more money for the next ten months.

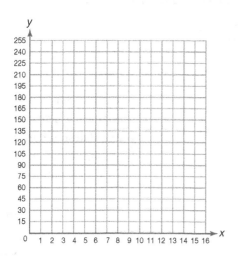

2 Mathias earns $9 an hour for babysitting.

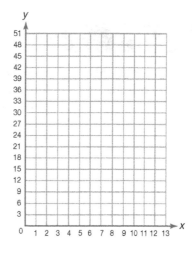

The table and graph represent two different linear functions. Which function has a greater rate of change?

x	−3	−1	0	1	3
y	−5	−1	1	3	7

1 **Determine the rate of change for the function in the table.**

Select any two ordered pairs from the table.

Using (3, 7) and (1, 3):

$\dfrac{\text{change in } y\text{-values}}{\text{change in } x\text{-values}} = \dfrac{7-3}{3-1} = \dfrac{4}{2} = 2.$

2 **Determine the rate of change for the function in the graph.**

Select any two points from the graph.

Using (0, −1) and (2, 5):

$\dfrac{\text{change in } y\text{-values}}{\text{change in } x\text{-values}} = \dfrac{5-(-1)}{2-0} = \dfrac{6}{2} = 3.$

3 **Compare the rates of change.** Since $3 > 2$, the rate of change is greater for the function represented by the graph.

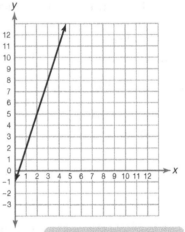

I see! I can compare slopes to compare the rates of change of linear functions.

 DISCUSS Dominic is comparing the rates of change of two positive linear functions by their graphs. How can he use the steepness of the lines to compare them? Explain.

LESSON LINK

PLUG IN ▸ **POWER UP** ▸ **GO!**

You can describe functional relationships from graphs.

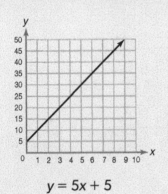

$y = 5x + 5$

You can sketch a graph of a functional relationship given a verbal description.

Sally earns $10 an hour as a math tutor.

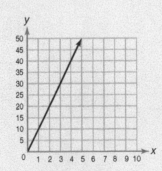

I get it! I can compare functional relationships given a verbal description, a graph, a table, or an equation.

WORK TOGETHER

Use coordinate grids to show which function has a greater y-intercept.

- Plot the points for each function.

- Draw the line for each function.

- Compare the y-intercepts.

The second function has a greater y-intercept.

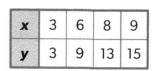

x	3	6	8	9
y	−1	2	4	5

x	3	6	8	9
y	3	9	13	15

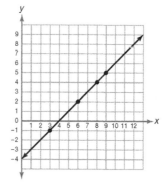

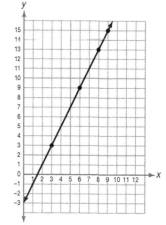

If I'm comparing linear functions written as equations, I can always look at the value of b in $y = mx + b$.

The y-intercept of the first function is −4.
The y-intercept of the second function is −3.
$-4 < -3$

A You can compare the rates of change of functions.

DO

Determine which function has a greater rate of change.

1 Determine the rate of change from the graph.

2 Determine the rate of change from the equation.

3 Compare the rates of change.

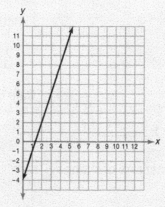

$y = 5x - 10$

Use two coordinate pairs from the graph: (0, −4) and (2, 2).

$$\frac{\text{change in } y\text{-values}}{\text{change in } x\text{-values}} = \frac{\boxed{} - \boxed{}}{\boxed{} - \boxed{}} = \frac{\boxed{}}{\boxed{}} = \boxed{}.$$

In the equation, $y = 5x - 10$, the rate of change is _____.

Since _____ > _____, the _____ has the greater rate of change.

Marjorie asks how she could compare linear functions whose graphs are horizontal lines. What would you tell her?

PRACTICE

Determine which function has a greater rate of change.

1 Function 1:

x	−2	−1	2	5
y	−6	−3	6	15

Rate of change for Function 1: _____

Function 2:

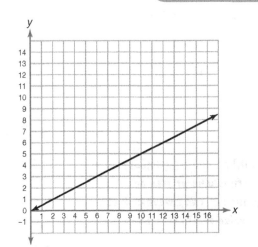

Rate of change for Function 2: _____

Function _____ has a greater rate of change.

2 Function 1:

x	−3	0	3	6
y	−3	0	3	6

Rate of change for Function 1: _____

Function _____ has a greater rate of change.

Function 2:

$y = \frac{1}{3}x + 2$

Rate of change for Function 2: _____

3 Function 1:

The output of this function is equal to the input multiplied by 10.

Rate of change for Function 1: _____

Function _____ has a greater rate of change.

Function 2:

$y = 15x - 25$

Rate of change for Function 2: _____

Determine which function has a greater y-intercept.

4 Function 1:

x	−2	0	1	3
y	−11	−5	−2	4

Function 2:

The output of this function is equal to 3 less than the product of the input and 2.

y-intercept for Function 1: _____

y-intercept for Function 2: _____

Function _____ has a greater y-intercept.

Compare functions based on their descriptions.

5 Which function has a greater rate of change? _____

Function 1: The output of this function is equal to 6 more than the product of the input and five.

Function 2: The output of this function is equal to 6 less than the product of the input and three.

That's right! The rate of change is the number being multiplied by the input.

6 Which function has a greater y-intercept? _____

Function 1: The output of this function is equal to 12 less than the product of the input and five.

Function 2: The output of this function is equal to 12 more than the product of the input and three.

 DISCUSS

Reason quantitatively.

Sonya says that the graph has a greater rate of change than the table because 4 > 3.

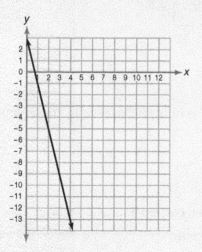

I need to make sure I calculate the slope of a line correctly from a graph to know its rate of change.

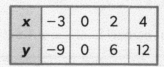

x	−3	0	2	4
y	−9	0	6	12

Do you agree with Sonya? Explain.

PROBLEM SOLVING

SUMMER JOBS

READ
Patricia and Allen each worked jobs during the summer. Patricia was paid $8 an hour. Allen created this table showing the number of hours he worked and the amount he was paid. Who was paid at a greater rate?

x	5	15	20	25	30
y	40.50	121.50	162.00	202.50	243.00

PLAN
• What is the problem asking you to find?

You need to find who was paid at a _____ rate.

• What do you need to solve the problem?

Patricia's pay rate: _____

Calculate Allen's pay rate by using the values in the table.

• How can you find Allen's pay rate?

By calculating the _____

SOLVE
Write an equation for Patricia's pay rate.

$y = \underline{\quad 8 \quad} x$

The rate of change is _____.

Find Allen's pay rate.

 $= \boxed{}$

The rate of change is _____.

> I remember! I can find the rate of change by choosing two ordered pairs and then finding the ratio of the change in y to the corresponding change in x!

CHECK
Multiply Allen's pay rate by some of the hours he worked to check your answer.

_____ × 20 = _____

_____ × 30 = _____

Patricia earned $_____ an hour. Allen earned $_____ an hour.

_____ was paid at a greater rate.

PRACTICE

Use the problem-solving steps to help you.

1 Eli jogged at a rate of 3 miles per hour. Taylor recorded his own distances and times in a table.

x	3	6	9	12
y	10.5	21	31.5	42

Who jogged at a faster rate?

2 Macie completed 10 multiplication problems a minute. Alexis made a graph showing the relationship between the number of multiplication problems she solved and how long it took her in minutes.

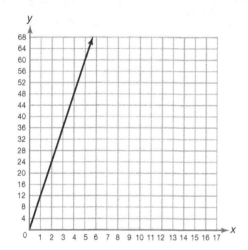

Who completed the problems at a faster rate?

3 Alec deposits the same amount of money each month into his savings account. He uses this equation to calculate the amount of money he has in his savings account: $y = 50x + 200$, after x months.

Shaelyn started her savings account with $250 and deposits $30 each month into her savings account.

Who saves money at a faster rate?

I can write an equation from a verbal description. Then it'll be easier to identify the slope!

Translations on a Coordinate Grid

Understanding Translations

A **rigid motion** changes the location of a figure.

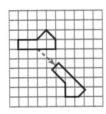

The names of points in the **image** of a transformation are shown using a prime symbol (').

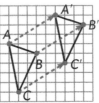

A **translation** slides a figure to a new location.

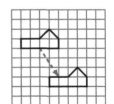

I get it! I can think of any change in a figure that keeps its size or shape as a rigid motion.

Ah! The symbol tells me whether points belong to the image or to the original figure. It also lets me know how the points correspond to each other.

I get it! In a translation, every point in a figure moves the distance in the same direction.

Words to Know

rigid motion
a transformation of a figure in a plane so that its size and shape are unchanged

image
the figure that results from a transformation

translation
a rigid motion in which a figure and its image have the same orientation

DISCUSS How is an angle changed by a translation?

A You can determine if a transformation is a translation.

DO Determine if one figure in the grid is a translation of the other figure.

❶ Find the number of units to the left or right and the number of units up or down between each point on the figure and the corresponding point on the figure's image.

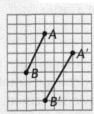

Are corresponding points the same direction and distance apart? _____

This _____ a translation.

❷ Identify a transformation as a translation if corresponding points are the same direction and distance apart.

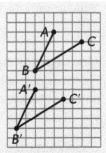

Are corresponding points the same direction and distance apart? _____

This _____ a translation.

I remember! A translation is a just slide to a new place.

B Translated segments are the same length and always parallel.

DO Determine if $\overline{AB}$ and $\overline{A'B'}$ are the same length and are parallel.

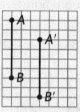

① Find the length of the original segment.

② Find the length of the image of the segment.

③ Find the slope of each segment.

Segment $\overline{AB}$ is _____ units long.

Segment $\overline{A'B'}$ is _____ units long.

Both segments have no slope.

Since two lines that have the same slope are parallel, $\overline{AB}$ and $\overline{A'B'}$ are _____.

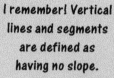

I remember! Vertical lines and segments are defined as having no slope.

DISCUSS Two segments have different lengths. Is it possible that one is a translation of the other? Explain.

PRACTICE

Determine if each transformation *is* or *is not* a translation.

①

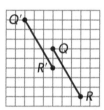

This _____ a translation.

②

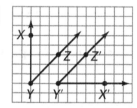

This _____ a translation.

Complete the translation of the figure given one point of the image.

③

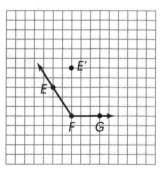

④

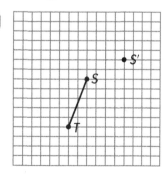

Translations and Congruence

Congruent figures have the same size and shape.

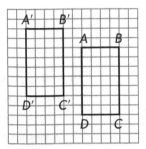

The **corresponding sides** of congruent figures are congruent.

ABCDEF ≅ PQRSTU

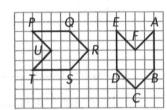

So corresponding side lengths of congruent figures have the same measure.

The **corresponding angles** of congruent figures are congruent.

$\overline{PQ} \cong \overline{AB}$	$\angle P \cong \angle A$
$\overline{RS} \cong \overline{CD}$	$\angle Q \cong \angle B$
$\overline{TU} \cong \overline{EF}$	$\angle R \cong \angle C$

I get it! Congruent figures can have different positions.

Words to Know

congruent (the symbol for "is congruent to" is ≅) having the same size and shape, but possibly different orientations

corresponding sides the sides of two figures that are in the same relative position

corresponding angles the angles of two figures that are in the same relative position

DISCUSS Are all circles congruent? Explain.

A You can find a translation that shows two figures are congruent.

DO Describe the translation showing that ABC and A'B'C' are congruent.

① Choose any vertex in the figure.

② Count the units along gridlines to the corresponding vertex of the image.

③ Describe the movements in a sentence.

A vertex is an endpoint of any segment that makes a figure.

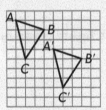

Each vertex of the image is _____ units to

the _____ and _____ units _____ from

the corresponding vertex of the original figure.

△A'B'C' is the image of △ABC translated

_____.

B You can use your understanding of translations to show that two figures are not congruent.

> For a transformation of a figure to be a translation, all points move the same distance and direction.

DO Determine if △ABC and △A′B′C′ are congruent.

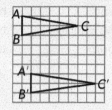

1 Determine the translation of one vertex.

2 Repeat for the remaining vertices.

3 Conclude whether the figures are congruent by comparing the translations of each vertex.

Point A moves _____ to the _____ and _____ units _____.

Point B moves _____ to the _____ and _____ units _____.

Point C moves _____ to the _____ and _____ units _____.

Each vertex _____ translated the same distance

and direction, so △ABC is _____ to △A′B′C′.

DISCUSS Roger says that these scalene triangles are not congruent because the distances between each vertex and its image are not the same for all vertices. How can you show Roger that he is not correct?

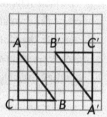

PRACTICE

Describe the translation that shows the two figures are congruent.

1

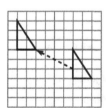

2

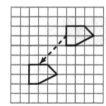

_____

_____

Use the notion of a translation to show that the two figures are not congruent.

3

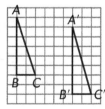

Because the vertex _____ is not

a translation like the others, △ABC

is _____ to △A′B′C′.

4

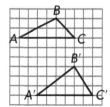

Because the vertex _____ is not

a translation like the others, △ABC

is _____ to △A′B′C′.

Translations in the x-y plane involve adding to and subtracting from the x and y coordinates of a figure.

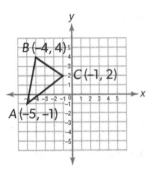

$(x, y) \rightarrow (x + 6, y - 3)$

> The rule tells me that each point of the translated figure is 6 units to the right and 3 units down from the corresponding point of the original figure.

Substitute the coordinates of each vertex into the rule to find the location of its translation.

$A(-5, -1) \rightarrow A'(-5 + 6, -1 - 3) \rightarrow A'(1, -4)$

$B(-4, 4) \rightarrow B'(-4 + 6, 4 - 3) \rightarrow B'(2, 1)$

$C(-1, 2) \rightarrow C'(-1 + 6, 2 - 3) \rightarrow C'(5, -1)$

> I see! I substitute the coordinates of each vertex into the rule to find the coordinates of the translated vertex.

Plot the image vertices and join them with segments that are images of the sides of the original figure.

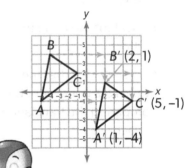

> I get it! The rule would let me translate any point of a figure, not just its vertices!

 DISCUSS   Why can the same rule be used for each point being translated?

LESSON LINK

PLUG IN

Translations change the location of figures without changing their size or orientation.

POWER UP

Translations produce congruent figures.

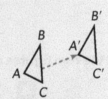

$\triangle ABC \cong \triangle A'B'C'$

GO!

> I see! Now I can carry out translations in the x-y plane and use rules to calculate the coordinates of images.

WORK TOGETHER

Use the rule $(x, y) \rightarrow (x - 2, y + 5)$ to translate the figure.

- Write the coordinates of the figure's vertices.

- Find the *x*- and *y*-values of the image's vertices using the rule.

- Plot the image vertices and draw the image.

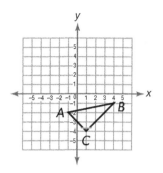

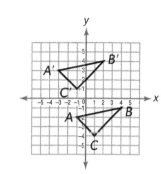

To subtract a negative number, I can add its opposite.

$A(-1, -2)$, $B(4, -1)$, $C(1, -4)$

$A(-1, -2) \rightarrow A'(-1 - 2, -2 + 5)$
$\rightarrow A'(-3, 3)$

$B(4, -1) \rightarrow B'(4 - 2, -1 + 5)$
$\rightarrow B'(2, 4)$

$C(1, -4) \rightarrow C'(1 - 2, -4 + 5)$
$\rightarrow C'(-1, 1)$

A You can write a rule for a translation.

DO

Find the rule for translating *ABC* to *A'B'C'*.

1. Choose any vertex in the figure.

2. Find the change in the *x*-coordinates and the change in the *y*-coordinates for a corresponding vertex in the image.

3. Make sure the change in each of the pairs of corresponding points is the same.

4. Write the rule.

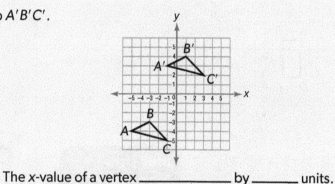

The *x*-value of a vertex _____ by _____ units.

The corresponding *y*-value of the vertex _____

by _____ units.

To form the image, the *x*-values of each point

_____ by _____ units and the

corresponding *y*-values _____ by

_____ units.

$(x, y) \rightarrow (x\text{\_\_\_\_\_}, y\text{\_\_\_\_\_})$

DISCUSS

Why is addition of a positive number used to translate to the right or upward?
Why is subtraction of a positive number used to translate to the left or downward?

PRACTICE

Translate the figure as specified by the rule.

1 $(x, y) \rightarrow (x + 4, y - 5)$

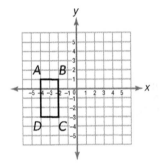

2 $(x, y) \rightarrow (x - 2, y + 1)$

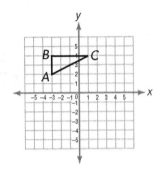

REMEMBER
Use the rule to find each coordinate of the vertices of the image.

3 $(x, y) \rightarrow (x + 6, y + 2)$

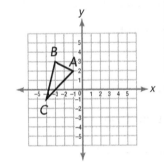

4 $(x, y) \rightarrow (x - 3, y - 6)$

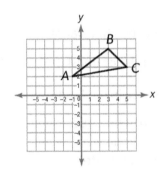

5 $(x, y) \rightarrow (x + 5, y)$

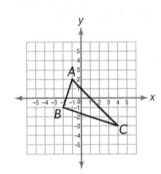

HINT
Sometimes only one of the coordinates increases or decreases.

6 $(x, y) \rightarrow (x, y + 3)$

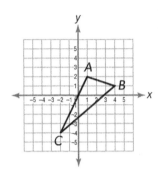

Write the rule for each translation.

7

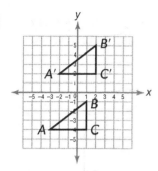

_____

8

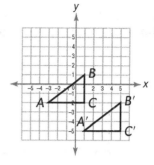

_____

9

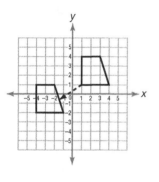

_____

10

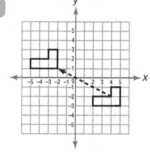

_____

Write the rule for the translation described.

I get it! If only one coordinate changes, the figure moves only vertically or horizontally.

11 3 units to the right   _____

12 5 units down   _____

 DISCUSS

See the Relationship and Make a Connection.

How is translating a figure on *x-y* coordinate axes like adding and subtracting using a number line? How is it different?

I can think about a comparison by drawing points on a number line and coordinates axes.

PROBLEM SOLVING

FURNITURE ARRANGEMENT

READ

Jim draws a diagram on a grid to show how he moved the desk in his office. Write a translation rule to describe how he moved his desk.

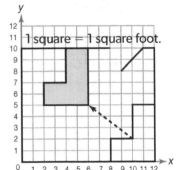

1 square = 1 square foot.

PLAN

- What are you asked to do? Describe how he moved

  his _____.

- What information do you need? The location of his desk

  _____ and _____ the move.

- How do you solve the problem? Find the _____ in the

  x- and y-values of the _____ vertices of the desk.

SOLVE

Find the coordinates of a vertex of the original position of the desk.

The coordinates of the bottom right vertex are (___**12**___, _____).

Find the coordinates of the corresponding vertex of the new position of the desk.

The corresponding coordinates are (_____, _____).

The x-coordinate _____ by _____.

The y-coordinate _____ by _____.

Jim moved the desk _____ feet to the left and _____ feet up.

CHECK

Find the change in the other vertices. Make sure the changes in the x- and y-values for the remaining corresponding vertices are the same.

(8, 0) → (_____, _____)

(12, 5) → (_____, _____)

(10, 5) → (_____, _____)

(10, 2) → (_____, _____)

(8, 2) → (_____, _____)

> The scale tells me that 1 square on the graph is equal to one square foot. That means the side of each square is equal to one foot.

The rule for the change in the location of the desk is (x, y) → (x _____, y _____).

PRACTICE

A quick sketch can help you understand the translation.

Use the problem-solving steps to help you.

1 Jason drew a diagram of his room on a grid. Each square on the grid is equal to one square foot. His desk is 11 squares down and 6 squares to the right of the window. Write a translation rule for moving the desk to the window.

CHECKLIST
- [ ] READ
- [ ] PLAN
- [ ] SOLVE
- [ ] CHECK

2 Triangle QRS is drawn on a coordinate grid where $Q(-3, 2)$, $R(6, 1)$, and $S(3, -4)$. Michelle draws its image, $\triangle Q'R'S'$, on the same coordinate grid using the translation rule $(x, y) \rightarrow (x - 6, y + 1)$. What are the coordinates of $\triangle Q'R'S'$?

CHECKLIST
- [ ] READ
- [ ] PLAN
- [ ] SOLVE
- [ ] CHECK

3 Maxine drew a map on a coordinate grid. Maxine's house is located at (7, 12). The distance on the map between Maxine's house and her friend's house can be described by the translation rule $(x, y) \rightarrow (x - 3, y + 2)$. What are the coordinates on the map of Maxine's friend's house?

CHECKLIST
- [ ] READ
- [ ] PLAN
- [ ] SOLVE
- [ ] CHECK

4 Jorge noticed a bug walking on a coordinate grid he drew on a piece of graph paper. He first sees the bug when it is at (7, 3). The bug crawls in a straight line to (1, −2). Write the bug's path as a translation rule.

CHECKLIST
- [ ] READ
- [ ] PLAN
- [ ] SOLVE
- [ ] CHECK

Reflections on a Coordinate Grid

PLUG IN · Understanding Reflections

A **reflection** is a flip of a figure over line.

The grid shows a segment and its reflection. If you fold the grid along the **line of reflection**, the two line segments will match exactly.

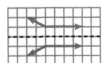
I see! When the paper is folded, the blue line segment aligns with the red line segment.

∠PQR is reflected over a line to form an image. The image of the reflection of point P is named with a prime symbol, P'.

Each point and its reflection are the same distance from the line of reflection.

2 units   2 units

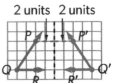

I get it! Points P and P' are each 2 units from the line of reflection.

Words to Know

reflection
a flip of a figure over a line

line of reflection
the line over which a figure is reflected

line of reflection

DISCUSS

Segment CD is reflected over a vertical line to form $\overline{C'D'}$. If you reflect $\overline{C'D'}$ over the same line, what will the image look like? Explain.

A You can reflect a segment over a line by finding the distance from each endpoint to the line.

DO Reflect $\overline{MN}$ over the dashed line to form $\overline{M'N'}$.

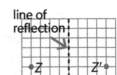

❶ Reflect point M over the line.

❷ Reflect point N over the line.

❸ Connect the points to form the reflected image, $\overline{M'N'}$.

Point M is _____ units to the _____ of the line of reflection.

So plot point M' _____ units to the _____ of the line of reflection.

Point N is _____ units to the _____ of the line of reflection.

So plot point N' _____ units to the _____ of the line of reflection.

$\overline{M'N'}$ is the reflection of $\overline{MN}$.

B You can reflect an angle over a line by finding the distance from each labeled point to the line.

 Reflect ∠XYZ over the dashed line.

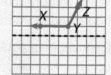

1 Reflect point X over the line.

2 Reflect point Y over the line.

3 Reflect point Z over the line.

4 Draw $\overrightarrow{Y'X'}$ and $\overrightarrow{Y'Z'}$ to form the image, ∠X'Y'Z'.

Point X is _____ unit(s) _____ the line of reflection. So plot point X'

_____ unit(s) _____ the line of reflection.

Point Y is _____ unit(s) _____ the line of reflection.

So plot point Y' _____ unit(s) _____ the line of reflection.

Point Z is _____ unit(s) _____ the line of reflection.

So plot point Z' _____ unit(s) _____ the line of reflection.

∠X'Y'Z' is the reflection of ∠XYZ.

C You can draw a line of reflection to show how figures can be reflected.

> I know my line is correct because I could fold the grid over the line and the segments would match up.

 Draw a line that could be used to reflect blue line segment $\overline{LM}$ so it aligns with the red segment $\overline{JK}$.

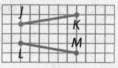

1 Find the distances between the corresponding endpoints.

2 Draw a line of reflection halfway between the corresponding endpoints.

The distance between J and L is _____ unit(s).

The distance between K and M is _____ unit(s).

One half of 2 is _____. So start a line that is _____ unit(s) above L.

One half of 4 is _____. So continue the line so that it is _____ unit(s) above M.

PRACTICE
Reflect the figure across the line.

1 Reflect $\overline{FG}$ to form $\overline{F'G'}$.

Draw a line of reflection.

2

When a figure is reflected across a line, the original figure and its image are congruent.

Each angle of △ABC is reflected, forming a congruent angle. So the corresponding angles of △A'B'C' are congruent.

The sides of a polygon are line segments.

Each line segment of △ABC is reflected, forming a congruent line segment. So the corresponding sides of △A'B'C' are congruent.

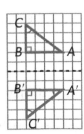

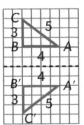

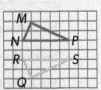

The reflection of right angle B is right angle B'. The angles are congruent!

So I know two figures are congruent when they are reflections of each other.

DISCUSS How can two triangles be congruent if one of them is flipped and faces the other direction?

A You can use a reflection to show that two triangles are congruent.

DO Draw a line of reflection to show that △MNP and △QRS are congruent.

❶ Find the distances between the corresponding vertices.

❷ Draw a line of reflection halfway between the corresponding vertices.

❸ Describe the reflection.

The distance between N and R is _____ unit(s).

The distance between M and Q is _____ unit(s).

The distance between P and S is _____ unit(s).

One half of 2 is _____. So start a line that is _____ unit(s) above R.

One half of 6 is _____. So continue the line so that it is _____ unit(s) above Q.

One half of 2 is _____. So continue the line so that it is _____ unit(s) above S.

△MNP is the reflection of △_____ over this line. This shows that the triangles are congruent.

I see! All corresponding angles are right angles, and all corresponding sides have the same lengths.

B You can reflect a figure to construct a congruent figure.

DO

Reflect rectangle *FGHJ* over the line to form a congruent rectangle.

1 Reflect points *G* and *H* over the line.

2 Reflect points *F* and *J* over the line.

3 Connect the points to form a rectangle.

Points *G* and *H* are each _____ unit(s) to the _____

of the line. So plot points *G'* and *H'* so each is _____

unit(s) to the _____ of the line.

Points *F* and *J* are each _____ unit(s) to the _____

of the line. So plot points *F'* and *J'* so each is _____

unit(s) to the _____ of the line.

Because rectangle *F'G'H'J'* is a reflection of rectangle

FGHJ, the figures are _____.

DISCUSS

If a segment is parallel to the line of reflection, what do you know about the image of the segment?

PRACTICE

Describe a line of reflection in words to show that the two figures are congruent. Then draw the line of reflection.

1

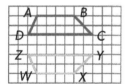

2

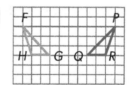

Reflect quadrilateral *ABCD* across the dashed line to form quadrilateral *A'B'C'D'*.

3

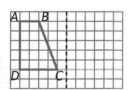

4

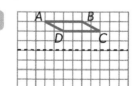

You can reflect figures on a coordinate plane and identify the coordinates of the vertices of the image.

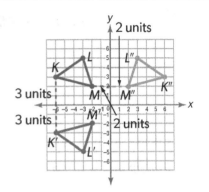

1 **Plot the image of the figure reflected across one axis.**
Reflect △KLM across the x-axis to form △K′L′M′. Point K is 3 units above the x-axis, so point K′ is 3 units below the x-axis.

2 **Find the coordinates of the vertices of the image.**
Record the vertices of △K′L′M′ from the graph.
K′(−6, −3)   L′(−3, −5)   M′(−2, −2)

3 **Compare the coordinates of the figure and its image to find a rule for a reflection over the x-axis.**
$(x, y) \rightarrow (x, -y)$

4 **Plot the image of the figure reflected across the other axis.**
Reflect △KLM across the y-axis to form △K″L″M″. Point M is 2 units to the left of the y-axis, so point M″ is 2 units to the right of the y-axis.

5 **Find the coordinates of the vertices of the image.**
Read the vertices of △K″L″M″ from the graph.
K″(6, 3)   L″(3, 5)   M″(2, 2)

6 **Compare the coordinates of the figure and its image to find a rule for a reflection over the y-axis.**
$(x, y) \rightarrow (-x, y)$

> I see! Each axis can be a line of reflection.

DISCUSS A point is plotted at the origin. What are the coordinates of its image if the point is reflected over the x-axis or y-axis? How do you know?

LESSON LINK

PLUG IN	**POWER UP**	**GO!**
I can reflect line segments and angles across a line.	I can reflect a figure across a line to form a congruent figure.	I get it! I can apply what I know about reflecting figures to graph congruent images on the coordinate plane.

WORK TOGETHER

You can reflect △FGH across the y-axis by plotting the images of the vertices. Then you can determine their coordinates.

- **Reflect vertex F of △FGH over the line**.
  Vertex F is 3 units to the left of the y-axis. Point F′ should be 3 units to the right of the y-axis.

- **Reflect vertex G over the line.** Point G′ should be 1 unit to the right of the y-axis.

- **Reflect vertex H over the line**. Point H′ should be 6 units to the right of the y-axis.

- **Connect the points to form △F′G′H′**. Identify and label the coordinates.

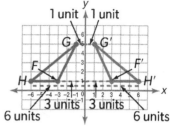

A You can use reflections to show that two triangles are congruent.

I see! To reflect a figure over the x-axis or y-axis, I can plot points and then find the coordinates. Or I can use a rule to find the coordinates and then plot them.

DO

Describe a sequence of reflections to show that △ABC is congruent to △TUV.

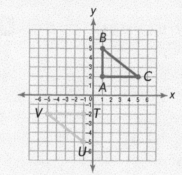

1 Find the coordinates of the reflection of A, B, and C over the y-axis. Plot and connect the points.

2 Find the coordinates of the reflection of A′, B′, and C′ over the x-axis.

3 Determine if the reflection(s) indicate congruence.

Apply the rule for a reflection over the y-axis.

$(x, y) \rightarrow (-x, y)$ 　　 $A(1, 2) \rightarrow A′(-1, 2)$

　　　　　　　　　 $B(1, 5) \rightarrow B′(-1, 5)$

　　　　　　　　　 $C(5, 2) \rightarrow C′(-5, 2)$

Apply the rule for a reflection over the x-axis.

$(x, y) \rightarrow (x, -y)$ 　　 $A′(-1, 2) \rightarrow A″(-1, -2)$

　　　　　　　　　 $B′(-1, 5) \rightarrow B″(-1, -5)$

　　　　　　　　　 $C′(-5, 2) \rightarrow C″(-5, -2)$

The coordinates of △ A″B″C″ are the coordinates of the vertices of △TUV. So a reflection across the y-axis followed by a reflection across the x-axis

shows that △_____ is congruent to △_____.

DISCUSS

Can figures on a coordinate plane be reflected over lines other the x-axis and the y-axis? Explain.

PRACTICE

Graph each reflection. Give the coordinates of the vertices of the image.

1 Reflect △ABC over the x-axis to form △A'B'C'.

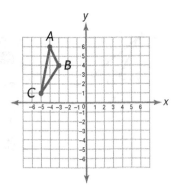

REMEMBER
The distance from corresponding vertices to the x-axis should be the same.

Coordinates: A'(_____, _____),

B'(_____, _____), C'(_____, _____)

2 Reflect △DEF over the y-axis to form △D'E'F'.

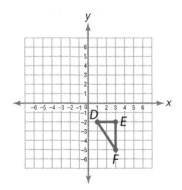

Coordinates: D'(_____, _____),

E'(_____, _____), F'(_____, _____)

3 Reflect trapezoid JKLM over the x-axis to form trapezoid J'K'L'M'.

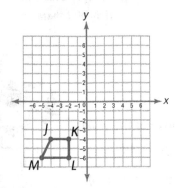

Coordinates: J'(_____, _____),

K'(_____, _____), L'(_____, _____),

M'(_____, _____)

4 Reflect triangle STV over the line x = 6 to form triangle S'T'V'.

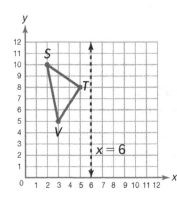

HINT
Find the distance from each vertex to x = 6. Then plot the image the same distance on the other side of the line.

Coordinates: S'(_____, _____),

T'(_____, _____), V'(_____, _____)

Describe a reflection or a sequence of reflections that could be used to show that quadrilateral ABCD is congruent to quadrilateral MNPQ.

5

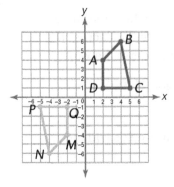

_____

_____

_____

_____

Talia used math software to create the quadrilateral labeled Drawing 1.

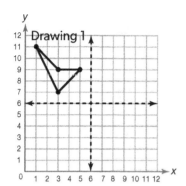

6 How can Talia flip her figure if she wants it to look like this?

_____

7 How can Talia flip her figure if she wants it to look like this?

_____

I can reflect Drawing 1 over the dashed lines to see how the images look.

DISCUSS

Look for a Pattern

Javier drew a triangle on the coordinate plane. He reflected the triangle over the x-axis. Then he reflected the image across the y-axis. Complete the coordinates of the reflections.

Reflection across the x-axis:

A(3, 4) → A′(3, −4)

B(2, 7) → B′(2, −7)

C(−3, 2) → C′(_____, _____)

Reflection across the y-axis:

A′(3, −4) → A″ (−3, −4)

B′(2, −7) → B″ (−2, −7)

C′(−3, −2) → C″ (_____, _____)

Write the rule for reflecting a point (x, y) over the x-axis and then reflecting its image over the y-axis.

PROBLEM SOLVING

MIRROR, MIRROR

READ

Rosa created this letter V on a coordinate grid. She wants to hold a mirror against the grid so the letter and its reflection look like the letter X. Draw a line to show where she should hold the mirror on the grid to create the letter X. Draw the image.

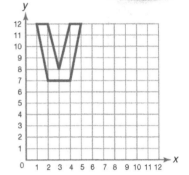

PLAN

• Find the location of the line of reflection over which V could be flipped so that the letter and its image create the letter _____.

• Use the drawing of the _____ on the coordinate plane to help solve the problem.

• Use trial and error to determine the horizontal or _____ line of reflection.

SOLVE

Try drawing a vertical line of reflection along the line $x = 5$.

Reflect the V over that line. Does it look like an X? _____

Try drawing a horizontal line of reflection along the line $y = 7$.

Reflect the V over that line. Does it look like an X? _____

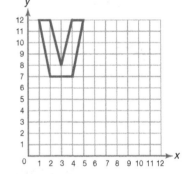

CHECK

To check your answer, compare the distances of each vertex with its image.

(1, 12) and (_____,_____) are both _____ units from $y = 7$.

(2, 7) and (_____,_____) are both _____ units from $y = 7$.

(4, 7) and (_____,_____) are both _____ units from $y = 7$.

(5, 12) and (_____,_____) are both _____ units from $y = 7$.

(4, 12) and (_____,_____) are both _____ units from $y = 7$.

(3, 8) and (_____,_____) are both _____ units from $y = 7$.

(2, 12) and (_____,_____) are both _____ units from $y = 7$.

Corresponding vertices are the same _____ from the _____, so the image is the reflection of the original figure.

If the mirror is placed along the line _____, the original figure and its reflection will form an X.

PRACTICE

Use the problem-solving steps to help you.

1 Ian created this letter L on grid paper. He wants to hold his letter up against a mirror so that it looks like the letter U. Draw a line to show how he should hold the mirror against the letter to create a U shape. Draw the image.

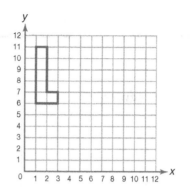

CHECKLIST

☐ READ

☐ PLAN

☐ SOLVE

☐ CHECK

2 Keitaro draws a diagram to decide where to move furniture in his house. The diagram shows the location of a rug in a living room. He wants to flip the rug over so it is in the new location shown. Draw the line of reflection he could use.

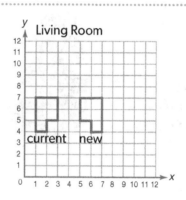

CHECKLIST

☐ READ

☐ PLAN

☐ SOLVE

☐ CHECK

3 Stella is using drawing software to make a product logo. The design uses a figure and its reflection as shown. Draw a line of reflection between the figure and its reflection.

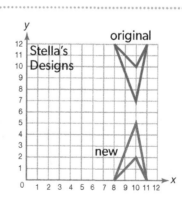

CHECKLIST

☐ READ

☐ PLAN

☐ SOLVE

☐ CHECK

12 Rotations on a Coordinate Grid

PLUG IN Understanding Rotations

A **rotation** is a turn around a point. Each point on the figure is rotated the same degree and direction of rotation around the **center of rotation** to form the image.

90°-Counterclockwise Rotation

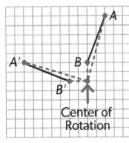

Center of Rotation

You can rotate angles around a point, too.

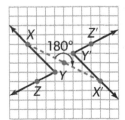

In any rotation, the measure of the angle formed by joining corresponding points to the center of rotation is equal to the degree of rotation.

Ah! The grid helps me to see that each point and its image are the same distance from the center of rotation.

I remember! A 180° angle is a straight line. So this angle has been rotated 180° to form the image.

Words to Know

rotation	center of rotation
a turn of a figure around a point	the point around which a figure is rotated

DISCUSS How many 90° rotations around the same center of rotation does it take for a figure to return to its original position? Explain.

A You can rotate line segments around a point.

DO Rotate the figure 180° counterclockwise around point *C*.

❶ Draw a 180° angle from point *A* through the center of rotation, *C*.

❷ Find the directions from the center of rotation to Point *A*. Then rotate these directions 180°.

❸ Repeat the process to place and label point *B'*. Draw a line connecting points *A'* and *B'*.

Point *A* is 3 units to the right and 4 units down from *C*.

Rotate these directions 180°. Plot point *A'* 3 units to the left and 4 units up from *C*.

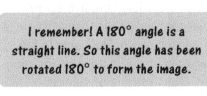

I see! A line from each point to its image would pass through the center of rotation.

B You can rotate angles around a point.

 Rotate the figure 90° counterclockwise around the center, *C*.

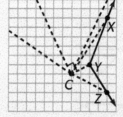

1 Connect point *X* to the center of rotation, *C*.

2 Move counterclockwise and draw a second line from the center of rotation to form a 90° angle with the first line.

3 Find the directions from *C* to point *X*. Then rotate these directions 90° counterclockwise to plot point *X'*.

Point *X* is 4 units to the right and 6 units up from *C*. Rotate these directions 90° clockwise. Plot point *X'* 6 units to the left and 4 units up from *C*.

4 Repeat the process to place and label points *Y'* and *Z'*.

5 Draw rays from point *Y'* through points *X'* and *Z'* to complete the image.

DISCUSS Describe a difference between a rotation and a translation.

PRACTICE

Draw the image for each rotation.

1 Rotate line segment *F'G'* 90°-counterclockwise around point *C*.

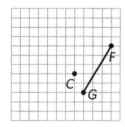

2 Rotate angle *R'S'T'* 180° around point *C*.

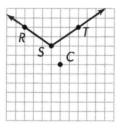

3 Rotate angle *L'M'N'* 90°-counterclockwise around point *N*.

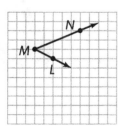

Two figures are **congruent** if they are the same size and shape.

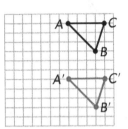

Rotating a figure does not change the size or shape of the original figure.

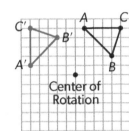

Center of Rotation

The distance between two points of the figure is equal to the distance between two corresponding points of the image. So rotated figures are congruent.

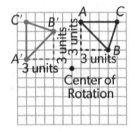

Center of Rotation

I see that the corresponding sides are the same lengths, so I know these two triangles are congruent.

These two triangles are still congruent, even though the second triangle has been rotated.

I see! The distance between points A and B is the same for both figures.

congruent
having the same size and shape, but possibly different orientations; indicated by the symbol ≅

DISCUSS   Donna wants to show that two figures on a grid are congruent. How might she use rotation to show this?

A You can create a congruent figure by rotation.

DO   Rotate △XYZ 180° around point C.

I remember. I find the directions from the center of rotation to point X. Then I rotate these directions 180° to plot point X'.

❶ Draw a 180° angle from vertex X through the center of rotation, C.

❷ Point X is 1 unit to the right and 1 unit down from C, so plot point X' 1 unit to the left and 1 unit up from C.

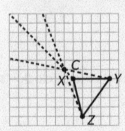

❸ Repeat the process to plot vertices Y' and Z'.

❹ Draw lines connecting point X' to Y', Y' to Z', and Z' to X'.

XYZ is _____ to X'Y'Z'.

B You can use a rotation to determine if two figures are congruent.

DO

Use rotation to show that figure *JKLM* is congruent to figure *QRST*.

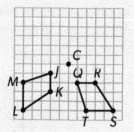

❶ Describe and compare the positions of corresponding vertices from the center of rotation, *C*.

❷ If the corresponding vertices of the figures are the same distance from the center of rotation, *C*, the two figures are congruent.

Q: to the right 1, down 2 from *C*

J: to the left 2, down 1 from *C*

R: to the right _____, down _____ from *C*

K: to the left _____, down _____ from *C*

S: to the right _____, down _____ from *C*

L: to the left _____, down _____ from *C*

T: to the right _____, down _____ from *C*

M: to the left _____, down _____ from *C*

JKLM is _____ to *QRST*.

DISCUSS

Triangle *ABC* is rotated around point *C* to form the image *A'B'C'*. If *A* and *A'* are the same distance from *C*, and *B* and *B'* are the same distance from *C*, how do you know that *ABC* and *A'B'C'* are congruent?

PRACTICE

1 Draw an image congruent to triangle *EFG* that is rotated 90°-counterclockwise around point *C*.

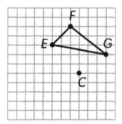

2 Describe the positions of corresponding vertices from the center of rotation, *C*, to determine if *PQRS* ≅ *TUVW*.

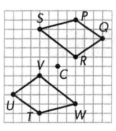

P: to the right _____, up _____ from *C*   *R*: to the right _____, up _____ from *C*

T: to the left _____, down _____ from *C*   *V*: to the left _____. down _____ from *C*

Q: to the right _____, up _____ from *C*   *S*: to the left _____, up _____ from *C*

U: to the left _____. down _____ from *C*   *W*: to the right _____. down _____ from *C*

Each corresponding vertex of the two figures is the _____ from the center of rotation.

PQRS is _____ to *TUVW*.

Rotations on a Coordinate Grid

When figures are plotted on a coordinate plane, the origin can be used as the center of rotation.

Every 90° a figure is rotated around the origin moves each point in the figure to an adjacent **quadrant**.

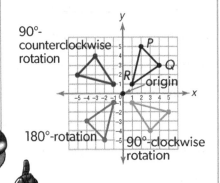

90°-counterclockwise rotation

origin

180°-rotation

90°-clockwise rotation

You can use a rule to find the coordinates of the vertices of an image from a rotation around the origin.

Rotate 90° clockwise:
$$(x, y) \rightarrow (y, -x)$$

Rotate 180°:
$$(x, y) \rightarrow (-x, -y)$$

Rotate 90° counterclockwise:
$$(x, y) \rightarrow (-y, x)$$

I remember! The origin has the coordinates (0, 0).

I see! A 180° rotation is the same clockwise or counterclockwise.

I see that the sign changes for at least one coordinate in each rule.

Words to Know

quadrant
one of the four sections of the *x-y* coordinate plane

DISCUSS Two vertices of a triangle are located in quadrant I and the third is on the origin. If the triangle is rotated 90° clockwise around the origin, what do you know about the coordinates of the image?

LESSON LINK

PLUG IN	POWER UP	GO!

You can rotate a figure around a point to create an image.

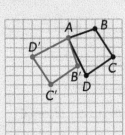

A rotated figure is congruent to the original figure.

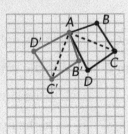

I see! I can use a coordinate grid to rotate figures around a point and determine the coordinates of the congruent image.

WORK TOGETHER

Use the pattern to rotate △ABC 180° around the origin.

- Identify the coordinates of each vertex.

- Use a rule to find the coordinates of the corresponding vertices of the image.

- Plot the vertices of the image.

- Connect the vertices to complete the image.

Vertices of △ABC:
$A(-5, 5), B(2, 3), C(-4, -1)$

180° rotation:
$(x, y) \rightarrow (-x, -y)$

$A(-5, 5) \rightarrow A'(5, -5)$

$B(2, 3) \rightarrow B'(-2, -3)$

$C(-4, -1) \rightarrow C'(4, 1)$

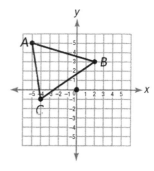

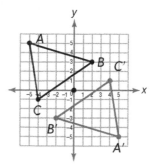

I see! When I rotate a figure 180° around the origin, both of the coordinates of the image's vertices are the opposites, or additive inverses, of the coordinates of the original vertices.

A Rotate a figure around the origin to create a congruent figure in the coordinate plane.

DO

Rotate ABCD 90° counterclockwise around the origin to construct a congruent figure.

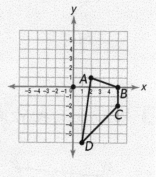

❶ Identify the coordinates of each vertex.

Vertices of ABCD: $A(2, 1), B(5,0),$
$C(5, -2),$ and $D(1, -6)$

❷ Use a rule to find the coordinates of the corresponding vertices of the image.

90°-counterclockwise rotation:
$(x, y) \rightarrow (-y, x)$

$A(\underline{\quad}, \underline{\quad}) \rightarrow A'(\underline{\quad}, \underline{\quad})$

$B(\underline{\quad}, \underline{\quad}) \rightarrow B'(\underline{\quad}, \underline{\quad})$

❸ Plot and label the vertices of the image.

$C(\underline{\quad}, \underline{\quad}) \rightarrow C'(\underline{\quad}, \underline{\quad})$

❹ Connect the vertices to complete the image.

$D(\underline{\quad}, \underline{\quad}) \rightarrow D'(\underline{\quad}, \underline{\quad})$

ABCD is $\underline{\qquad}$ to A'B'C'D'.

DISCUSS

Julio is rotating a quadrilateral 180°. The vertices of the quadrilateral are $(7, 7), (-4, 8), (-3, -1),$ and $(6, -1)$. He says that the coordinates of the image vertices are: $(7, -7), (8, 4),$ $(-1, 3),$ and $(-1, -6)$. What can you tell him about his work?

I know! I can use the rules for rotating by different degrees to check the rotation.

PRACTICE

Draw the image for each rotation.

1 Rotate $\overline{ST}$ 90° clockwise around the origin.

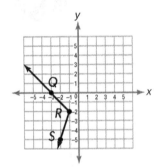

> **REMEMBER**
> The vertices of the image must be labeled on the coordinate grid.

2 Rotate $\overline{AB}$ 90° clockwise around the origin.

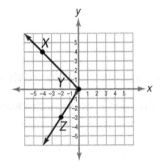

3 Rotate angle QRS 90° counterclockwise around the origin.

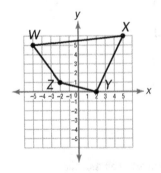

4 Rotate angle XYZ 180° around the origin.

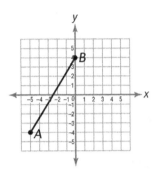

5 Rotate figure WXYZ 180° around the origin.

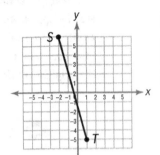

6 Rotate △XYZ 90° clockwise around the origin.

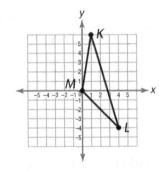

> **HINT**
> Check your rotation by making sure the figure and its image have the same size and shape.

Use rotation around the origin to identify the two figures as *congruent* or *not congruent*.

7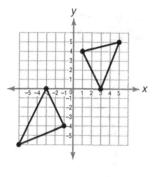

_____

8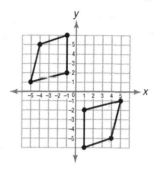

_____

9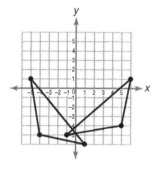

_____

10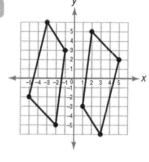

_____

 Use Logical Reasoning

Haley draws the point A in the first quadrant of a coordinate grid. She draws the image A′ by rotating A 90° clockwise about the origin. She then draws the image A″ by reflecting A across the x-axis. Will A′ and A″ always have the same coordinates? Explain.

Try transforming different points on a coordinate grid using rotation and reflection to compare their images.

PROBLEM SOLVING

MAPS AND ROTATIONS

READ A landscaper plots points on a coordinate grid to show the location of flower beds in a garden. The first square flower bed is in Quadrant I. He finds the location of a second flower bed by rotating the first flower bed 90° counterclockwise around the origin. What will be the coordinates of the vertices of the second flower bed? Draw the second flower bed on the grid.

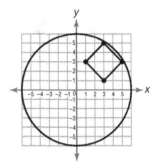

PLAN • To find the coordinates of the vertices of the second

flower bed, _____ the given figure

90° _____ around the origin.

• Use the coordinates of the _____ of the first flower bed and the

rule for finding the _____ of the image (the second flower bed).

SOLVE Find the coordinates of the original flower bed using the model.

(__3__, __1__); (_____, _____);

(_____, _____); (_____, _____)

State the rule for rotating a coordinate 90° counterclockwise about the origin.

$(x, y) \rightarrow$ (_____, _____)

Find the coordinates of the image of the flower bed.

(_____, _____) → (_____, _____)

(_____, _____) → (_____, _____)

Plot the coordinates on the map.

(_____, _____) → (_____, _____)

Connect the points to show the plant on the grid.

(_____, _____) → (_____, _____)

CHECK Rotate the image 90° clockwise. Use the vertices of the first image to find the vertices of the second image.

(_____, _____) → (_____, _____)

(_____, _____) → (_____, _____)

Rule for 90° clockwise rotation: $(x, y) \rightarrow (y, -x)$

(_____, _____) → (_____, _____)

(_____, _____) → (_____, _____)

Determine if the coordinates of the rotated second image match the coordinates of the original figure.

Rotating the vertices of the image 90° clockwise produces the original coordinates.

The coordinates of the second flower bed are:

(_____, _____), (_____, _____), (_____, _____), (_____, _____).

PRACTICE

Use the problem-solving steps to help you.

I see! The vertices of a figure and its image must be listed in the same order.

1 Riley creates a pattern on a coordinate grid. He draws 3 of the 4 parts of the pattern by forming congruent triangles by rotation. Triangle 1 has vertices at (0, 0), (−4, 5), and (−8, 3). Triangle 2 has vertices at (0, 0), (5, 4), and (3, 8). Triangle 3 has vertices at (0, 0), (4, −5), and (8, −3). If he continues the rotation pattern, what are the vertices of the fourth triangle?

CHECKLIST
- [ ] READ
- [ ] PLAN
- [ ] SOLVE
- [ ] CHECK

2 Arshad uses a coordinate grid to design a playground. The vertices of the figure representing the slide are at (5, 2), (5, 9), (6, 2), and (6, 9). The designer wants to place an identical slide in Quadrant III by rotating the figure representing the slide around the origin. What are the coordinates for the location of the second slide?

CHECKLIST
- [ ] READ
- [ ] PLAN
- [ ] SOLVE
- [ ] CHECK

3 Imari draws a coordinate grid on a whiteboard to demonstrate how to rotate a figure. He writes the vertices of the figure and its image on cards. Before he can attach the coordinates to his whiteboard, he drops his cards. He remembers that the figure was in Quadrant III. List the coordinates of the figure and its image. Then state in which quadrant the image will be located.

(−3,−1) (4, −5) (−1, −2) (1, −3) (−5, −4) (2, −1)

CHECKLIST
- [ ] READ
- [ ] PLAN
- [ ] SOLVE
- [ ] CHECK

13 Dilations on a Coordinate Grid

PLUG IN   Enlarging a Figure Using Dilations

A **dilation** is a transformation that changes the size of a figure.

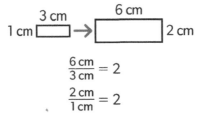

I see! In a dilation, the shape doesn't change, but the size does.

After a dilation, the measures of the corresponding sides of the figure and its image are proportional. When the **scale factor** is greater than 1, the dilation is an enlargement.

1 cm ▭ 3 cm → ▭ 6 cm 2 cm

$$\frac{6\ cm}{3\ cm} = 2$$

$$\frac{2\ cm}{1\ cm} = 2$$

The scale factor of this dilation is 2, so the image is larger than the figure.

Scale drawings are used in construction, engineering, and architecture to represent much larger or smaller things.

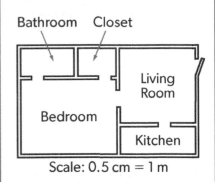

Scale: 0.5 cm = 1 m

I get it! The actual rooms are much larger than they are in this scale drawing.

dilation
a transformation that changes the size of a figure

scale factor
the ratio of the lengths of corresponding sides of a dilation

scale drawing
a drawing of a real object that has been enlarged or reduced by a scale factor

DISCUSS

Diane has a 4-inch by 6-inch photo. She prints two larger copies of the photo. One copy has a scale factor of 2. The other copy has a scale factor of 4. Which copy has a greater width? Explain.

A You can find the scale factor of a dilation and use it to find a missing side length.

DO Determine the scale factor for the dilation from △ABC to △XYZ and use it to find the missing length.

> I see! Each ratio of corresponding sides is equal to the scale factor.

1 Identify the corresponding sides of the two figures.

2 Write and simplify a ratio for the corresponding sides to find the scale factor.

3 Use the scale factor to find the missing length of $\overline{XZ}$.

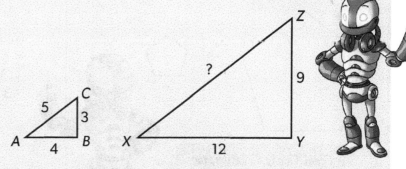

The corresponding sides are:

$\overline{XY}$ and $\overline{AB}$, $\overline{XZ}$ and _____, $\overline{ZY}$ and _____.

$\frac{XY}{AB}$ = _____ = _____

$\frac{ZY}{CB}$ = _____ = _____

The scale factor is _____.

5 × _____ = _____

The length of side XZ is _____ units.

DISCUSS Ron asks what a scale diagram would look like if he used a scale factor of 1.

PRACTICE

Figure B is a dilation of figure A. Find the scale factor.

1

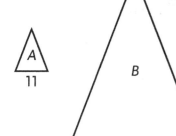

The scale factor is _____.

Figure B is a dilation of figure A using the given scale factor. Find the missing length.

2 Scale factor = $\frac{5}{2}$

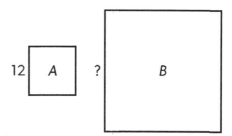

The length is _____ units.

A figure can also be reduced using a dilation.

I see! This is a dilation, too. The figure gets smaller, but it doesn't change shape.

When a scale factor is between 0 and 1, the dilation is a reduction.

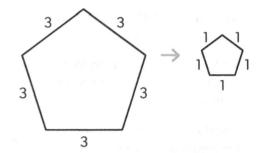

I get it! Each side of the new figure is $\frac{1}{3}$ the length of each side of the old figure. So the scale factor is $\frac{1}{3}$.

DISCUSS Mark makes a scale drawing of a T-shirt design. His scale drawing has dimensions that are $\frac{1}{2}$ of the actual dimensions of his design. He sends the drawing to a factory. It performs a dilation of 2 on the scale drawing to print the T-shirt. What happened to the figure at the factory?

A You can find the scale factor of a dilation and use it to find a missing length.

DO Determine the scale factor to dilate trapezoid *ABCD* to trapezoid *MNOP*.

1 Identify the corresponding sides of the two figures.

2 Write and simplify a ratio for the corresponding sides to find the scale factor.

3 Use the scale factor to find the length of side *MN*.

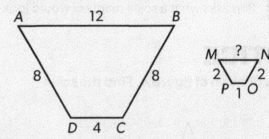

The corresponding sides are: __**MP**__ and __**AD**__,

$\overline{MN}$ and _____, $\overline{NO}$ and _____, _____ and _____.

$\dfrac{MP}{AD} =$ _____ $=$ _____ $\dfrac{NO}{BC} =$ _____ $=$ _____

$\dfrac{OP}{CD} =$ _____

The scale factor is _____.

$12 \times$ _____ $=$ _____

The length of side *MN* is _____.

B You can make a scale drawing using a dilation.

DO

Regina made a scale drawing of her living room to plan where to put her new furniture. The room is 15 feet by 12 feet, and the scale factor is $\frac{1}{60}$. Make a scale drawing of the living room.

Grid Paper can be found on page 217.

1 Multiply the scale factor by the length of each wall in the drawing.

Longer wall: _____ $\frac{1}{60}$ _____ · _____ **15** _____ ft = _____ ft

Shorter wall: _____ · _____ ft = _____ ft

2 Convert feet to inches.

Longer wall: _____ · 12 in. = _____ in.

3 Use grid paper and a ruler to draw the living room. Label the walls with the actual wall measurements.

Shorter wall: _____ · 12 in. = _____ in.

DISCUSS

Sarah makes a scale drawing of a car with a length of 3 meters and a width of 2 meters. She plans to use a scale factor of $\frac{1}{10}$. In the drawing, the car is 0.4 meter by 0.3 meter. What can you tell Sarah about her drawing?

PRACTICE

Figure *B* is a dilation of Figure *A*. Find the scale factor.

1

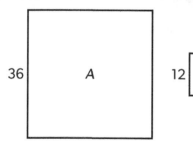

The scale factor is _____.

Figure *B* is a dilation of Figure *A* using the given scale factor. Find the missing length.

2

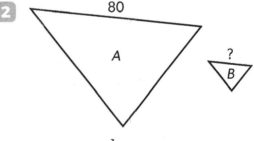

Scale factor: $\frac{1}{20}$
The length is _____ units.

Use grid paper and a ruler to make a scale drawing.

3 Rectangular pool

Length: 25 feet

Width: 15 feet

Scale Factor: $\frac{1}{100}$

4 Hexagon-shaped flower bed

Each side: 12 feet

Scale Factor: $\frac{1}{80}$

Grid Paper can be found on page 219.

You can show a dilation of a figure on a coordinate plane.

The vertices of the dilated figure are found by multiplying the coordinates of the vertices of the original figure by a scale factor.

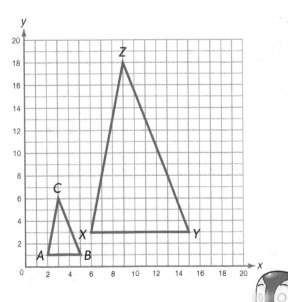

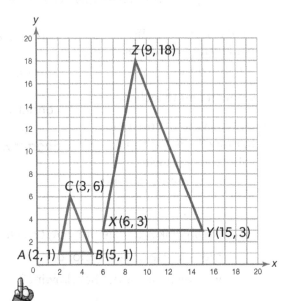

I see! The red triangle is smaller than the blue one, but they are the same shape.

I get it! When the coordinates of a vertex in the red triangle are multiplied by the scale factor 3, I get the coordinates of the corresponding vertex in the blue triangle.

DISCUSS When a figure is dilated on the coordinate plane, how does the value of the scale factor change its shape and size?

LESSON LINK

PLUG IN

POWER UP

GO!

You can enlarge a figure by multiplying its side lengths by a scale factor greater than 1.

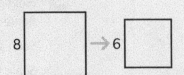

Scale factor = 1.5

$2 \times 1.5 = 3$

You can reduce a figure by multiplying its side lengths by a scale factor between 0 and 1.

Scale factor = $\frac{3}{4}$

$8 \times \frac{3}{4} = 6$

I get it! I can dilate figures on the coordinate plane by multiplying each of the coordinates by the scale factor.

WORK TOGETHER

You can use coordinate grids to determine if the blue triangle is an enlargement of the red triangle.

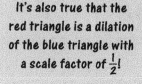
It's also true that the red triangle is a dilation of the blue triangle with a scale factor of $\frac{1}{2}$!

- List the coordinates of each figure.

- Find a constant scale factor between corresponding vertices.

- If the scale factor is consistent, the blue triangle is a dilation of the red triangle.

- The scale factor is 2.

- The blue triangle is an enlargement of the red triangle.

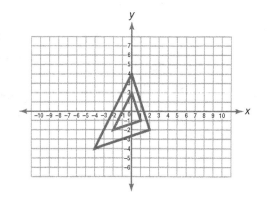

Red triangle: (−2, −2), (1, −1), (0, 2)

Blue triangle: (−4,−4), (2, −2), (0, 4)

Compare the coordinates of the vertices of the blue triangle with the coordinates of the vertices of the red triangle. Each coordinate of the blue triangle is two times the coordinate of the red triangle.

A You can calculate the coordinates of a reduced figure.

I see! I name the vertices in the order given in the problem to match the vertices of the original figure.

DO

Dilate triangle *LMN* by a scale factor of $\frac{1}{2}$ to create triangle *OPQ*. Use the origin as the center of dilation.

1 List the coordinates of the vertices of the original figure.

2 Multiply each coordinate of the original figure by the scale factor to find the coordinates of the dilated figure.

3 Plot and connect the vertices of the dilated figure.

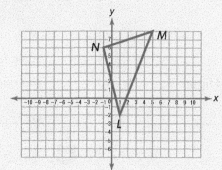

$L =$ **(1, −2)**, $M =$ _____, $N =$ _____

$O =$ _____, $P =$ _____, $Q =$ _____

DISCUSS

Gerald asks if figures on a coordinate grid with different numbers of sides can ever be dilations of each other. How would you respond?

PRACTICE

The blue figure is a dilation of the red figure. Find the scale factor.

1

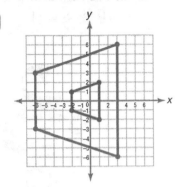

> **HINT**
> Find the ratios of the corresponding x-coordinates and y-coordinates.

The scale factor is _____.

2

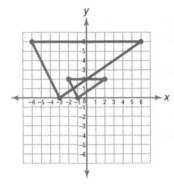

> **REMEMBER**
> If the figure is enlarged, the scale factor is greater than 1. If the figure is reduced, the scale factor is between 0 and 1.

The scale factor is _____.

Find the coordinates of the dilated figure.

3

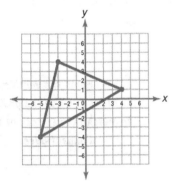

Scale factor is 3.

The coordinates of the dilated figure

are _____.

4

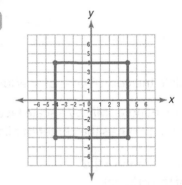

Scale factor is $\frac{1}{4}$.

The coordinates of the dilated figure

are _____.

5

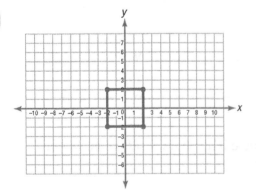

Scale factor is 5.

The coordinates of the dilated figure

are _____

and _____.

6

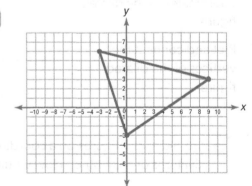

Scale factor is $\frac{1}{3}$.

The coordinates of the dilated figure

are _____.

Find the coordinates.

7 Connie plotted a quadrilateral on a coordinate grid. The quadrilateral had vertices at (−3, 2), (−4, 2), (−1, −2), and (−6, −2). She dilated the figure using a scale factor of 3. What are the coordinates of the vertices of the dilated figure?

8 Chris plotted a triangle on a coordinate grid. The triangle had vertices at (−2, 6), (−2, 0), and (2, 0). He dilated the figure using a scale factor of $\frac{1}{2}$. What are the coordinates of the vertices of the dilated figure?

9 Eric plotted two quadrilaterals on a coordinate grid. The red quadrilateral had vertices at (−4, 4), (12, 4), (8, −8), and (−4, −4). The blue quadrilateral had vertices at (−1, 1), (3, 1), (2, −2), and (−1, −1), respectively. If the blue quadrilateral is a dilation of the red quadrilateral, what scale factor did Eric use?

Determine if the described dilation is an enlargement or a reduction.

In an enlargement, the scale factor is greater than 1. In a reduction, the scale factor is between 0 and 1.

10 Sasha plotted two triangles on a coordinate grid. The red triangle had vertices at (−7, −5), (−2, −3), and (−6, 2). The blue triangle had vertices at (−3.5, −2.5), (−1, −1.5), and (−3, 1), respectively. The blue triangle is a dilation of the red triangle.

_____

11 Peter plotted two quadrilaterals on a coordinate grid. The red quadrilateral had vertices at (7, 0), (5, 4), (−2, 1), and (−5, 4). The blue quadrilateral had vertices at (21, 0), (15, 12), (−6, 3), and (−15, 12), respectively. The blue quadrilateral is a dilation of the red quadrilateral.

_____

I can sketch figures to see how transformations change a figure, but I don't need to use a coordinate grid here.

 See the Relationship

Translations, rotations, and reflections don't change the shape or size of a figure. Dilations can change the size, but not the shape. You can also combine transformations to create completely new figures.

If a figure is rotated and then reflected, will the size change? _____

If a figure is rotated and then dilated, will the size change? _____

What can you say about combining transformations and the size and shape of the image?

PROBLEM SOLVING

PICTURE PERFECT

READ

Beth prints out a photo of her dog, Belle. The photo is 8 inches by 5 inches. She would like to enlarge it so that it fits in a frame that is 48 inches by 30 inches. How can she enlarge the photo so that it fits the frame exactly?

PLAN

• What is the problem asking you to find?

the _____ for a dilation

• How can you find the scale factor of the picture frame?

_____

• Do you expect a scale factor greater than 1 or lesser than 1?

SOLVE

_____

Write and simplify the ratios of the corresponding sides of the photo and frame.

Length: $\frac{frame}{photo} = \frac{\boxed{48}}{\boxed{}} = $ _____

Width: $\frac{frame}{photo} = \frac{\boxed{30}}{\boxed{}} = $ _____

> I can work backwards to check my work. Instead of multiplying to find the dimensions of the enlargement, I can divide to find the dimensions of the original photo.

Are the ratios equal? _____

CHECK

What is the scale factor? _____

Is the scale factor greater than or less than 1? _____

Does this scale factor represent an enlargement or a reduction? _____

Divide the dimensions of the frame by the scale factor. What dimensions result?

_____

The photo can fit the frame by _____ by a scale factor of _____.

PRACTICE

Use the problem-solving steps to help you.

> The units of measurement do not matter as long as they are the same for all measurements.

1 Images on computer screens can be measured in units called pixels. A computer programmer reduces an image from 500 by 400 pixels to 450 pixels by 360 pixels. What scale factor did she use?

CHECKLIST

- ☐ READ
- ☐ PLAN
- ☐ SOLVE
- ☐ CHECK

2 Tess designs a small skateboard by reducing the size of a standard skateboard. A standard skateboard and her new skateboard are sketched on the coordinate plane. The factory that will produce the new skateboards needs the scale factor to be between $\frac{1}{2}$ and $\frac{3}{4}$. Will her design work? Explain.

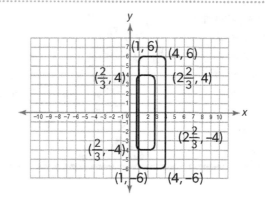

CHECKLIST

- ☐ READ
- ☐ PLAN
- ☐ SOLVE
- ☐ CHECK

3 A scale drawing shows the length and width of a car as 4 inches by 2 inches. If a scale factor of 30 was used to create the scale drawing, what is the actual length and width, in feet, of the car?

CHECKLIST

- ☐ READ
- ☐ PLAN
- ☐ SOLVE
- ☐ CHECK

14 Similarity

PLUG IN Congruent Figures

In congruent figures, corresponding angles and corresponding sides have the same measures.

When one figure is a rotation or reflection of another, the figures are congruent. The following triangles are congruent.

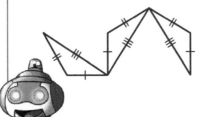

When one figure is a dilation of another, the figures are not congruent. The following triangles are not congruent.

I see! For corresponding side lengths, $a = d$, $b = e$, and $c = f$. And for corresponding angles,
$m\angle A = m\angle D$,
$m\angle B = m\angle E$
and $m\angle C = m\angle F$.
$\triangle ABC \cong \triangle DEF$

I remember! When I rotate and reflect a figure, the image is congruent.

That makes sense! When I dilate a figure, I change its size to produce an image.

DISCUSS

A triangle is translated on a coordinate grid. Are the original figure and its image congruent? Explain.

A You can use rigid motion(s) to show that figures are congruent.

DO

Show that $\triangle RTI$ and $\triangle RWO$ are congruent.

❶ What three ways can you move $\triangle TRI$ so its image will be congruent?

❷ Determine the motion whose image maps to $\triangle RWO$.

❸ Draw an arrow to show the motion.

❹ State the congruency.

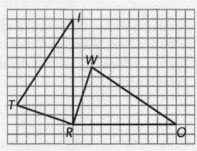

by _____, _____ or _____

$\triangle RTI$ is a _____

$\triangle RTI \cong \triangle$_____

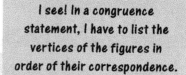

B You can use a series of rigid motions to show that figures are congruent.

 Show that trapezoid *ABCD* is congruent to trapezoid *LMNO*.

I see! In a congruence statement, I have to list the vertices of the figures in order of their correspondence.

❶ Use a reflection.

❷ Use a vertical translation.

❸ Use a horizontal translation.

❹ State the congruency.

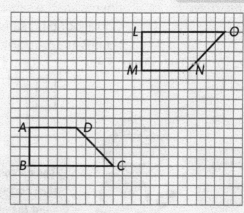

Reflect trapezoid *ABCD* along side _____.

Translate trapezoid *ABCD* _____ squares up.

Translate trapezoid *ABCD* _____ squares right.

trapezoid *ABCD* _____ trapezoid *LMNO*

PRACTICE

Name a rigid motions that can show that the shapes are congruent.

1
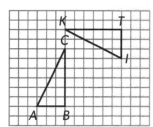

_____

2

_____

3
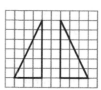

_____

Use rigid motions to show that the following figures are congruent. Draw and explain your steps.

4 △*CAB* ≅ △*KIT*

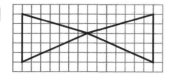

5 *THIS* ≅ *JUMP*

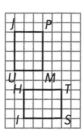

6 △*DOG* ≅ △*PET*

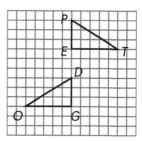

Similar figures have the same shape, but they may have different sizes.

Corresponding angles of similar figures are the same size. Corresponding sides of similar figures are proportional.

Similar figures can be created by rotation, reflection, translation, or dilation. All of the following triangles are similar.

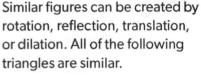

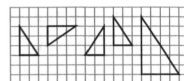

> I see! All circles have the same shape, but they can have different sizes. So all circles are similar.

> The corresponding angles of the rectangles are the same. And the sides of the larger rectangle are twice as long as the corresponding sides of the smaller rectangle.

> I see! I know triangles are similar by comparing proportions. Or I know they are similar if I can show they are congruent!

Words to Know

similar
having the same shape, but possibly having a different size; the symbol ~ means similar

DISCUSS

Layla says that similar shapes can sometimes be congruent too. Brandon disagrees. What do you think? Explain.

A You can prove figures are similar by proving they are congruent.

DO

Show that trapezoid *SHIP* is similar to trapezoid *PORT*.

1 Compare the sizes of the figures to determine if dilation is necessary.

2 Determine the rigid motions to show trapezoid *SHIP* is congruent to trapezoid *PORT*.

3 State the similarity.

The sizes are _____.

_____ trapezoid *SHIP*

90° clockwise around point

____ and then _____

_____ units _____.

The trapezoids _____ congruent.

trapezoid *SHIP* _____ trapezoid *PORT*

When I compare figures of different sizes, I can compare ratios to show similarity instead of determining a series of transformations.

B Use proportions to determine if two figures are similar.

DO

Compare side lengths to determine if rectangles *ABCD* and *EFGH* are similar.

1 Write ratios for pairs of corresponding sides.

2 State the similarity.

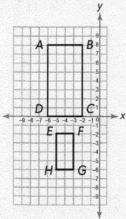

$$\frac{\text{longer side of } ABCD}{\text{longer side of } EFGH} = \frac{AD}{\boxed{}} = \frac{\boxed{}}{\boxed{}} = \underline{\quad}$$

$$\frac{\text{shorter side of } ABCD}{\text{shorter side of } EFGH} = \frac{\boxed{}}{\boxed{}} = \frac{\boxed{}}{\boxed{}} = \underline{\quad}$$

Corresponding sides are _____.

Rectangle *ABCD* is _____ to *EFGH*.

DISCUSS

Taylor says that congruent figures are similar figures whose corresponding side lengths have a ratio of 1. Do you agree? Explain.

PRACTICE

Name two transformations that can show the figures are congruent.

1 △*ACE* ~ △*LOW*

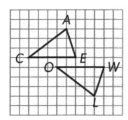

_____

△*ACE* ≅ △*LOW*, so △*ACE* is _____ to △*LOW*.

Use properties of similarity to determine if two figures are similar.

2

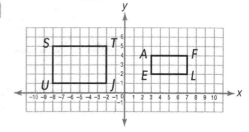

$$\frac{\text{longer side of } LEAF}{\text{longer side of } JUST} = \underline{\quad} = \underline{\quad} = \underline{\quad}$$

$$\frac{\text{shorter side of } LEAF}{\text{shorter side of } JUST} = \underline{\quad} = \underline{\quad} = \underline{\quad}$$

The sides _____ in proportion.

Rectangle *LEAF* is _____ to rectangle *JUST*.

137

You can use transformations that show the similarity of two figures.

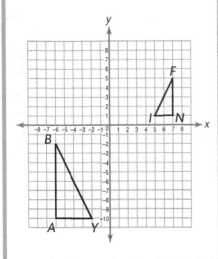

Compare side lengths to define the dilation.

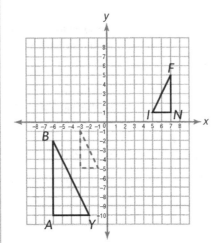

The side lengths of △FIN are half the length of the side lengths of △BAY.

Reflect the image over the y-axis, and translate the reflection until one vertex aligns with △FIN.

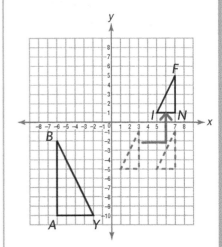

I see that the orientations of the figures are different.

I see! The vertex coordinates of the image are each one half times the vertex coordinates of the original figure!

I see! If I can describe a series of rigid motions and a dilation between figures, I know the two triangles are similar.

 DISCUSS On a scale drawing, the scale factor is the ratio of the lengths on the drawing to the actual lengths. How is a scale factor related to dilation of a figure used to prove similarity?

LESSON LINK

PLUG IN	POWER UP	GO!
You can use transformations to show that figures are congruent.	You can use proportions to show that figures are similar.	I get it! I can use what I've learned to show that figures are similar. I can describe rigid motions and dilations that show whether figures are similar.

WORK TOGETHER

You can use figures plotted on a grid to determine if rectangles *BENT* and *CAMP* are similar.

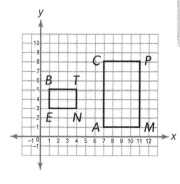

If I'd found the sides were proportional, I could have described dilation, along with rigid motions, to show that the rectangles are similar!

- Compare the proportions of the corresponding sides to describe the dilation.

- Consider what this tells about the rectangles.

$$\frac{\text{longer side of } BENT}{\text{longer side of } CAMP} = \underline{\hspace{1cm}} = \underline{\hspace{1cm}}$$

$$\frac{\text{shorter side of } BENT}{\text{shorter side of } CAMP} = \underline{\hspace{1cm}} = \underline{\hspace{1cm}} = \underline{\hspace{1cm}}$$

The proportions _____ the same.

Rectangles *BENT* and *CAMP* _____ similar

because the sides _____ proportional.

A You can describe transformations that show that two figures are similar.

DO Describe translations to determine if △*ZIP* is similar to △*NUM*.

1 The sizes of the figures are the same, so the transformations do not include dilation.

2 Describe the transformations that show the figures are similar.

3 State the similarity.

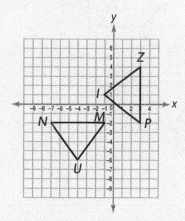

_____ △*ZIP* 90° _____ around point _____,

and then _____ units _____.

△*ZIP* is _____ to △*NUM*.

Huong says all congruent figures are similar, but not all similar figures are congruent. Is he correct?

PRACTICE

Describe transformations that can be used to determine whether the figures are similar.

1 Rectangles *FOUR* and *ALMS*

> **REMEMBER**
> Start by finding a proportion for dilation, followed by rigid motions that map one figure to another.

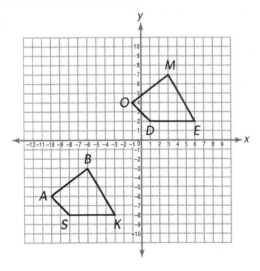

2 Rectangles *FAKE* and *NURS*

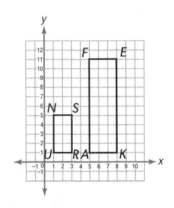

Describe the transformations that show these figures are similar.

3

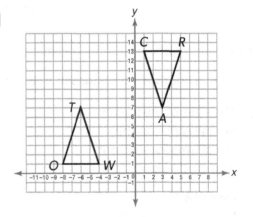

4

Describe dilations and other transformations that show whether the figures are similar.

5

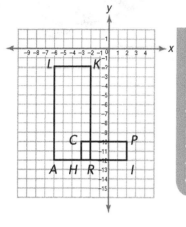

> **HINT**
> Dilating one figure to the same size as the other first makes it easier to determine the remaining translations.

6

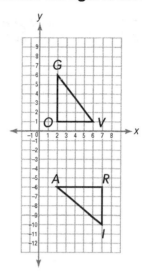

7

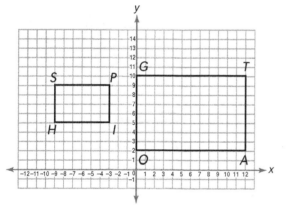

8

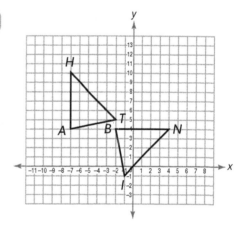

Look for Patterns

Zachary says he checks his transformations by performing them in reverse from the final figure to see if he returns to the original figure.

Maria says this doesn't work for her. She had dilated a figure by $\frac{1}{2}$ and then rotated it 90° clockwise. To check, she dilated the final figure by $\frac{1}{2}$ and rotated it 90° counterclockwise. She found the final figure wasn't the same as the original figure.

What did Maria do wrong?

PROBLEM SOLVING

GRAPHIC DESIGN

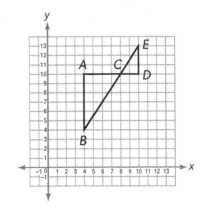

READ

Ashley is a graphic designer. She wants to make a logo that uses two similar triangles. Determine if her logo has two similar triangles.

PLAN

• What is the problem asking you to find?

   Are the triangles _____?

• What do you need to do to solve the problem?

   Describe the _____ used.

   Check for _____.

SOLVE

Identify the dilation and the rigid transformations.

Is △ABC similar to △DEC?

Find the dilation:

$\frac{DE}{AB} = \frac{CD}{CA} =$ _____

So dilate △ABC by a factor of _____.

Find the coordinates of the dilated image.

A(4, 10) → (_____, _____) B(4, 4) → (_____, _____) C(8, 10) → (_____, _____)

Describe the transformations: Translate the image _____ units to the _____ and _____

units _____.

Rotate the translation of the image around point _____ _____.

Grid Paper can be found on p. 225.

CHECK

To check your transformation of △ABC to △DEC, try to transform △DEC to △ABC.

Dilate △DEC by a factor of _____.

D(10,10) → (_____, _____) E(10,13) → (_____, _____) C(8,10) → (_____, _____)

To align the image of C to point C, translate 10 units down and 8 units to the left.

Rotate the translation around point _____ _____.

△ABC is _____ to △DEC.

PRACTICE

Use the problem-solving steps to prove whether the following figures are similar.

1 Matt creates a new wallpaper design. He will repeat this design in different colors. Describe transformations that show whether the two figures in the design are similar.

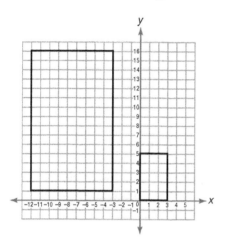

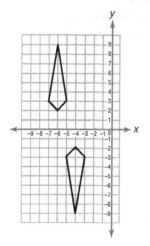

CHECKLIST
- [ ] READ
- [ ] PLAN
- [ ] SOLVE
- [ ] CHECK

2 Clover sees a pattern on her gift wrapping paper. This design is repeated in different directions. Describe transformations that show whether the shapes are similar.

CHECKLIST
- [ ] READ
- [ ] PLAN
- [ ] SOLVE
- [ ] CHECK

Angles in Triangles

PLUG IN Angle Pairs

Complementary angles have measures that add up to 90°.

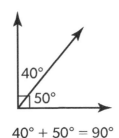

$$40° + 50° = 90°$$

Supplementary angles have measures that add up to 180°.

$$30° + 150° = 180°$$

> I get it! I can determine if two angles are complementary or supplementary angles by adding their angle measures.

Adjacent angles share a common side and a common vertex.

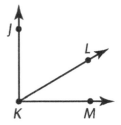

∠JKL and ∠LKM are adjacent angles.

Vertical angles are opposite angles formed by two intersecting lines. Vertical angles have the same measure.

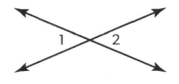

∠1 and ∠2 are vertical angles.

> I see that the lines that form vertical angles also form four pairs of adjacent angles!

Words to Know

complementary angles	supplementary angles	adjacent angles	vertical angles
angles whose measures add up to 90°	angles whose measures add up to 180°	angles that share both a common side and a common vertex	opposite angles formed by two intersecting lines

DISCUSS Can a pair of angles be described in more than one of these ways? (See **Words to Know**.) Explain.

A You can use the definition of complementary angles to find missing angle measures.

> **DO**
>
> What is the value of *a*?

1 Understand the problem.　The angles add up to _____°.

2 Write an equation to find *a*.　$15° + a = $ _____°

3 Solve.　$a = 90° - $ _____°

　　$a = $ _____°

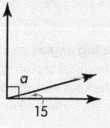

B You can use angle relationships to find missing angle measures.

> **DO**
>
> What is the value of *x*?

I remember! $m\angle AGR$ means "the measure of angle AGR."

1 Understand the problem.

$\angle AGR$ and $\angle$ _____ are vertical angles.

$m\angle SGT = $ _____

2 Write an equation to find the value of *x*.

$m\angle AGR = $ _____

$m\angle AGP + m\angle$ _____ $= m\angle AGR$

3 Solve the equation.

$48 + x = $ _____

$x = 90 - $ _____

$x = $ _____

The value of *x* is _____.

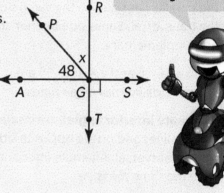

> **DISCUSS**
>
> Two lines intersect and form a pair of complementary vertical angles. What are the measures of each of these angles? How do you know?

PRACTICE

Use the diagram at the right for questions 1–4.

1 Name a pair of supplementary angles.

$\angle$ _____ and $\angle$ _____

2 Name a pair of complementary angles.

$\angle$ _____ and $\angle$ _____

3 Name a pair of adjacent angles.

$\angle$ _____ and $\angle$ _____

4 Name a pair of vertical angles.

$\angle$ _____ and $\angle$ _____

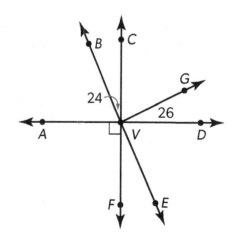

Angles Formed by a Transversal

Special angle pairs are formed when parallel lines are intersected by a transversal (a line that intersects two or more lines). In the diagrams below, line *j* and line *m* are parallel. Line *k* is a transversal.

Corresponding angles are on the same side of a transversal and on the same side of the parallel lines. Corresponding angles have the same measure.

$\angle1$ and $\angle5$, $\angle2$ and $\angle6$, $\angle4$ and $\angle8$, $\angle3$ and $\angle7$ are corresponding angle pairs.

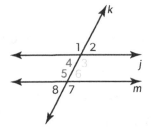

Same-side interior angles are between the parallel lines and on the same side of the transversal. Same-side interior angles are supplementary.

$\angle3$ and $\angle6$ and $\angle4$ and $\angle5$ are same-side interior angle pairs.

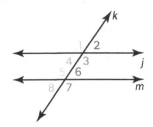

Wow! I can use these definitions to find the measures of angles formed by parallel lines and a transversal!

Alternate interior angles are inside the parallel lines and on the opposite sides of the transversal. Alternate interior angles have the same measure.

$\angle3$ and $\angle5$ and $\angle4$ and $\angle6$ are alternate-interior angle pairs.

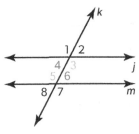

Alternate exterior angles are outside the parallel lines and on the opposite sides of the transversal. Alternate exterior angles have the same measure.

$\angle1$ and $\angle7$ and $\angle2$ and $\angle8$ are alternate exterior angle pairs.

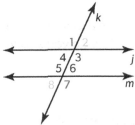

Words to Know	**corresponding angles** angles that are in the same position when a transversal intersects two parallel lines	**same-side interior angles** angles that are between two parallel lines and on the same side of the transversal	**alternate interior angles** angles that are between two parallel lines and on opposite sides of the transversal	**alternate exterior angles** angles that are outside two parallel lines and on opposite sides of the transversal

 DISCUSS What other special angle pairs do you see in the diagrams above?

A You can use what you know about angles formed by a transversal to find congruent angles.

DO

Line *a* is parallel to line *b*. Line *t* is a transversal. Identify all of the angles that are congruent to ∠1. Then identify all of the angles congruent to ∠2.

❶ Identify the angle pairs that have the same measure.

Which types of angles have the same measure?

_____

❷ List all of the angles that have the same measure as ∠1.

_____

$m\angle 1 = m\angle$ _____ $= m\angle$ _____ $= m\angle$ _____

❸ List all of the angles that have the same measure as ∠2.

$m\angle 2 = m\angle$ _____ $= m\angle$ _____ $= m\angle$ _____

I get it! *m* ∠1 means "the measure of angle 1."

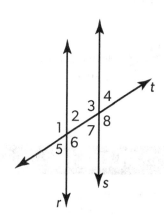

DISCUSS

Kiera says if she knows just one angle measure in a diagram with a pair of parallel lines and a transversal, she can find all of the other angle measures. Explain why Kiera is correct.

PRACTICE

Use the diagram to answer questions 1–6. Line *r* is parallel to line *s*. Line *t* is a transversal.

❶ ∠8 and ∠_____ are corresponding angles.

❷ ∠3 and ∠_____ are same-side interior angles.

❸ ∠5 and ∠_____ are alternate exterior angles.

❹ ∠6 and ∠_____ are alternate interior angles.

❺ Which angles have the same measure as ∠7?

$m\angle 7 = m\angle$ _____ $= m\angle$ _____ $= m\angle$ _____

❻ Which angles are supplementary to ∠6?

∠_____, ∠_____, ∠_____, ∠_____

147

Every triangle has three **interior angles**. The measures of the angles of a triangle add up to 180°.

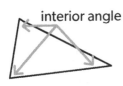

interior angle

Any side of a triangle can be extended, forming an **exterior angle** outside the triangle.

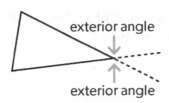

exterior angle

exterior angle

If two interior angles of two triangles are congruent, then the triangles are similar.

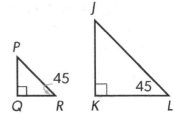

$m\angle Q = m\angle K = 90$

$m\angle R = m\angle L = 45$

$\triangle PQR$ is similar to $\triangle JKL$.

> I see! "Interior" means inside. Interior angles are inside the triangle.

> This makes sense. "Exterior" means outside, and exterior angles are outside of the triangle.

> I get it! Because two of the angles are congruent, the third one must also be congruent.

Words to Know

interior angle
an angle inside a polygon that is formed by two sides of a polygon

exterior angle
an angle outside of a polygon formed by extending one side of the polygon

DISCUSS How many exterior angles does a triangle have? How are they related to the interior angles? Explain.

LESSON LINK

PLUG IN	POWER UP	GO!

You can use the relationships of angle pairs to find their measures.

Other special angle pairs are formed when a transversal intersects parallel lines.

> I get it! I can use what I know about angle relationships to determine how the interior and exterior angles of triangles are related.

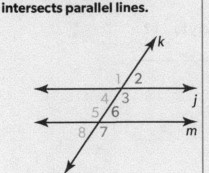

WORK TOGETHER

Determine the relationship of the exterior angle measures of a triangle.

- Find the sum of the exterior angle measures.

- Write a general statement about the measures of the exterior angles of a triangle.

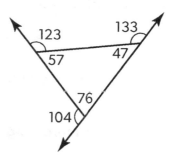

Wow! There are so many relationships angles can have!

$$123 + 133 + 104 = 360$$

The measures of the exterior angles of a triangle add up to 360°.

A You can determine if three angle measures can form a triangle.

DO

Can a triangle have interior angle measures of 67, 82, and 55? Explain.

1 Write the angle relationship for the sum of the angles in a triangle.

2 Write an equation that shows the sum of the angles described.

3 Answer the question.

The sum of the measures of the angles of a triangle is

_____.

$67 +$ _____ $+$ _____ $=$ _____

Angles that measure 67, 82, and 55

_____ be used to draw a triangle because

_____.

B You can compare angle measures to determine if two triangles are similar.

DO

Is △XYZ similar to △LMN? Explain.

1 Understand the problem.

2 List the labeled corresponding angles that are congruent.

3 Determine similarity.

If pairs of _____ angles of two triangles are congruent, then the triangles are similar.

∠X is congruent to ∠_____.

∠Z is congruent to ∠_____.

If two pairs of interior angles of two triangles are _____,

then the triangles are _____.

△XYZ _____ similar to △LMN.

 Susan says that all equilateral triangles are similar to each other. Is Susan correct? Explain.

PRACTICE

Find the angle measure to complete each sentence.

1 The exterior angle of an equilateral triangle measures _____.

2 If two angles of a triangle are complementary, the third angle measures _____.

Determine whether the following sets of interior angle measures form a triangle. Circle *yes* or *no*.

3 90, 90, 30   yes or no

> **REMEMBER**
> The interior angles of a triangle add up to 180°.

4 140, 24, 16   yes or no

Write an equation to find the value of the missing angle in each triangle. Show your work.

5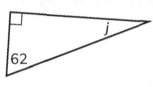

> **REMEMBER**
> A right angle is indicated by a square.

$m\angle j =$ _____

6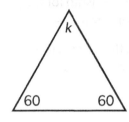

$m\angle k =$ _____

7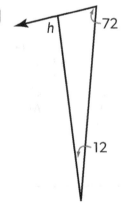

> **HINT**
> Sometimes you have to find more than one missing angle measure.

$m\angle h =$ _____

8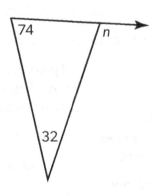

$m\angle n =$ _____

Find the value of y for each triangle.

 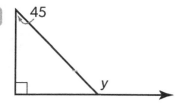

45

y

$m\angle y =$ _____

> I know that adjacent angles that form a straight line are supplementary, so their measures add up to 180°.

 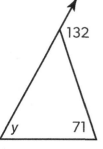

132

y   71

$m\angle y =$ _____

Determine whether the triangles are similar.

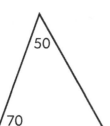 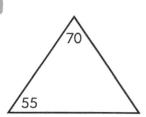

70   50

55   70

The triangles _____ similar.

DISCUSS

Construct an Argument

Lora says that the triangles at the right are similar. Show that Lora is correct.

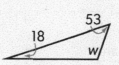 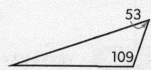

18   53   53

w   109

Find the value of w. $18 + 53 + w = 180$

$71 + w = 180$

$w = 180 - 71$

$w =$ _____

> I know! If I can show that at least two corresponding angles are congruent, then the triangles are similar.

Why are the triangles similar? _____

_____

151

PROBLEM SOLVING

CLIMB TO THE TOP

READ   Christopher and his grandfather place a ladder against
a wall to paint their roof. At what angle does the top
of the ladder meet the wall?

PLAN   • What do you need to know to solve the problem?

What is the angle between the wall and the ground? _____

What is the size of the other labeled angle? _____

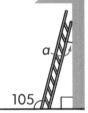

• How can you calculate the angle at the top of the ladder?   105

First, find the angle between the _____ and the ground.

Since the interior angle measures add up to 180°, use the other two angles to find the
measure of the top angle.

SOLVE   Find the measure of the interior angle formed by the bottom of the ladder and the ground.

$105 + x =$ _____

$x = 180 -$ _____

$x =$ _____

Find the measure of the angle formed by the top of the ladder and the house.

$75 + 90 + a =$ _____

_____ $+ a = 180$

$a = 180 -$ _____

$a =$ _____

CHECK   Work backward.

Find x.

$15 + 90 + x =$ _____

_____ $+ x = 180$

$x = 180 -$ _____

$x =$ _____

The angle formed by the top of the ladder and the wall is _____.

PRACTICE

Solve. Use the problem-solving steps to help you.

1 William and his brother are building part of a wooden house frame. What is the value of *x* in this diagram?

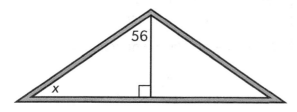

CHECKLIST
- [ ] READ
- [ ] PLAN
- [ ] SOLVE
- [ ] CHECK

$m\angle x =$ _____

2 Hailey draws this flag. The angles formed by the blue lines and the sides of the flag each measure 52°. What are the measures of the four angles formed at the intersection of the lines?

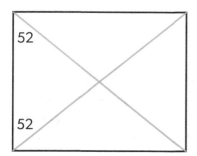

CHECKLIST
- [ ] READ
- [ ] PLAN
- [ ] SOLVE
- [ ] CHECK

3 A flagpole is supported by a wire that forms the exterior angle shown in the diagram. What are the values of *a*, *b*, and *c*?

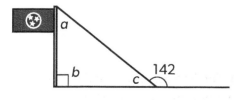

I see! I know one of these angles without calculating.

CHECKLIST
- [ ] READ
- [ ] PLAN
- [ ] SOLVE
- [ ] CHECK

$m\angle a =$ _____ $m\angle b =$ _____ $m\angle c =$ _____

16 Using the Pythagorean Theorem on a Coordinate Grid

PLUG IN Understanding the Pythagorean Theorem

In any right triangle, the sum of the squares of the lengths of the **legs** is equal to the square of the length of the longest side, called the **hypotenuse**. This is called the **Pythagorean theorem**.

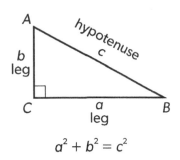

$$a^2 + b^2 = c^2$$

> I see! The hypotenuse is the side opposite the right angle. The legs are the two shorter sides.

You can use the converse of the Pythagorean theorem to prove that a triangle is a right triangle.

Determine if $\triangle ABC$ is a right triangle.

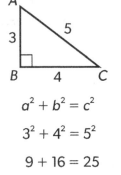

$$a^2 + b^2 = c^2$$
$$3^2 + 4^2 = 5^2$$
$$9 + 16 = 25$$
$$25 = 25 \checkmark$$

$\triangle ABC$ is a right triangle.

> I get it! The converse of the Pythagorean theorem says that if the sum of the squares of the lengths of the legs of a triangle is equal to the square of the hypotenuse, then the triangle is a right triangle.

Pythagorean theorem	**hypotenuse**	**legs**
In any right triangle, the sum of the squares of the lengths of the legs is equal to the square of the length of the hypotenuse.	the side opposite the right angle in a right triangle	the sides that form the right angle in a right triangle

DISCUSS Two side lengths of a triangle are 10 cm and 12 cm. The interior angles of the triangle are 60°, 40°, and 80°. Can you apply the Pythagorean theorem to find the length of the third side?

A You can use the converse of the Pythagorean theorem to determine if a triangle is a right triangle.

DO Is △DEF a right triangle?

① Identify the two possible legs and the possible hypotenuse.

② Apply the Pythagorean theorem.

③ Determine if the triangle is a right triangle.

$\overline{DE}$ is a _____.

$\overline{EF}$ is a _____.

$\overline{DF}$ is the _____.

$a^2 + b^2 = c^2$

_____^{2} + _____^{2} $\overset{?}{=}$ _____^{2}

_____ + _____ $\overset{?}{=}$ _____

_____ ◯ _____

Is △DEF a right triangle? _____

PRACTICE

Determine whether the triangle is a right triangle.

1

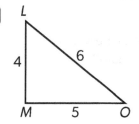

□^{2} + □^{2} $\overset{?}{=}$ □^{2}

□ + □ $\overset{?}{=}$ □

□ ◯ □

Is the triangle a right triangle? _____

2

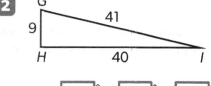

□^{2} + □^{2} $\overset{?}{=}$ □^{2}

□ + □ $\overset{?}{=}$ □

□ ◯ □

Is the triangle a right triangle? _____

3 A triangle with one side 13″ long and two sides 9″ long.

Is the triangle a right triangle? _____

4 A triangle with sides 9″, 12″, and 15″

Is the triangle a right triangle? _____

You can use the Pythagorean theorem to find unknown side lengths.

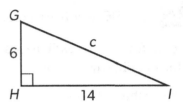

1. Determine which measures are given and which measure is unknown.

2. Substitute the given values into the Pythagorean theorem. Let c represent the length of the hypotenuse.

3. Solve the equation for the unknown value. Round to the nearest tenth, if necessary.

The lengths of the legs are 6 and 14. The length of the hypotenuse is unknown.

$$a^2 + b^2 = c^2$$
$$6^2 + 14^2 = c^2$$
$$36 + 196 = c^2$$
$$232 = c^2$$
$$\sqrt{232} = \sqrt{c^2}$$
$$15.2 \approx c$$

The length of the hypotenuse is about 15.2.

> I see! Since c is squared, I have to take the square root of each side.

DISCUSS   Carl draws a square and then draws a diagonal from opposite vertices. If he knows the length of the diagonal, how can he determine the side length of the square?

A   You can use the Pythagorean theorem to find the length of one leg.

DO   Find the length of $\overline{KL}$.

1. Determine which measures you know and which you don't know.

2. Substitute the known values into the Pythagorean theorem. Let b represent the length of the other leg.

3. Solve the equation for the unknown value. Round to the nearest tenth, if necessary.

The length of one leg is 17, and the length of the hypotenuse is 25. The length of the other leg is unknown.

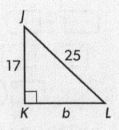

$$a^2 + b^2 = c^2$$
$$\boxed{}^2 + b^2 = \boxed{}^2$$
$$\boxed{} + b^2 = \boxed{}$$
$$b^2 = \boxed{}$$
$$\sqrt{b^2} = \sqrt{\boxed{}}$$
$$b \approx \boxed{}$$

The length of $\overline{KL}$ is about _____.

B You can use the Pythagorean theorem to solve problems.

DO

A 15-foot ladder is resting at an angle against a wall. The bottom of the ladder is 9 feet from the wall. How high up the wall is the top of the ladder?

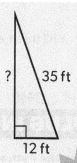

15 ft   b

9 ft

1 Determine which measures you know, and which you don't know.

The length of one leg is 9, and the length of the hypotenuse is 15. The length of the other leg is unknown.

2 Substitute the known values into the Pythagorean theorem. Let b represent the length of the other leg.

$a^2 + b^2 = c^2$

$\boxed{}^2 + b^2 = \boxed{}^2$

3 Solve the equation for the unknown value. Round to the nearest tenth, if necessary.

$\boxed{} + b^2 = \boxed{}$

$b^2 = \boxed{}$

$\sqrt{b^2} = \sqrt{\boxed{}}$

$b = \boxed{}$

The top of the ladder is _____ feet up the wall.

DISCUSS

Grace was asked to find the missing side length for the triangle.

This is how she started.
$a^2 + b^2 = c^2$
$35^2 + 12^2 = c^2$

What can you tell Grace about her work?

?   35 ft

12 ft

PRACTICE

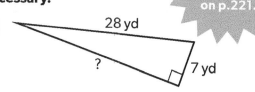

Pythagorean Theorem Proof can be found on p. 221.

Find the missing length. Round to the nearest tenth, if necessary.

1

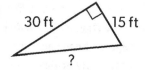

30 ft   15 ft

?

The length of the hypotenuse is about

_____ feet.

2

28 yd

?   7 yd

The length of the longer leg is about

_____ yards.

Using the Pythagorean Theorem on a Coordinate Grid

You can use the Pythagorean theorem to solve problems on the coordinate grid.

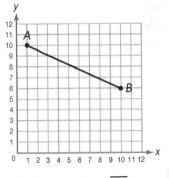

What is the length of $\overline{AB}$?

> I can draw a right triangle and then use the Pythagorean theorem.

Add legs to make a right triangle. Determine the lengths of each leg.

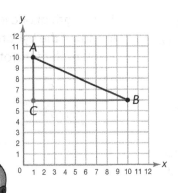

> I can find the lengths of $\overline{AC}$ and $\overline{CB}$ by counting the units.

Use the length of the legs to find the length of the hypotenuse.

Length of $\overline{AC}$ = 4 units

Length of $\overline{CB}$ = 9 units

$a^2 + b^2 = c^2$

$4^2 + 9^2 = c^2$

$16 + 81 = c^2$

$97 = c^2$

$c = \sqrt{97}$

$c = 9.848...$

AB is about 9.8 units.

> I can round the length to the nearest tenth, when necessary.

 DISCUSS   Will this method work for segments whose endpoints are in different quadrants? Explain.

LESSON LINK

| **PLUG IN** | **POWER UP** | **GO!** |

You can use the Pythagorean theorem to prove that a triangle is a right triangle.

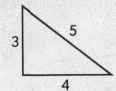

$a^2 + b^2 = c^2$
$3^2 + 4^2 = 5^2$
$9 + 16 = 25$
$25 = 25$

This is a right triangle.

You can use the Pythagorean theorem to find the length of an unknown side.

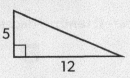

$a^2 + b^2 = c^2$
$5^2 + 12^2 = c^2$
$25 + 144 = c^2$
$169 = c^2$
$13 = c$

> I get it! I can apply the Pythagorean theorem in other problem situations, like finding the lengths of segments on coordinate grids!

WORK TOGETHER

Find the length of $\overline{DE}$.

- Add legs along the grid lines to make a right triangle with the given segment as the hypotenuse.

- Count squares to find the length of each leg.

- Use the Pythagorean theorem.

Length of $\overline{DF}$ = 10 units

Length of $\overline{EF}$ = 4 units

$$a^2 + b^2 = c^2$$
$$10^2 + 4^2 = c^2$$
$$100 + 16 = c^2$$
$$116 = c^2$$
$$c = \sqrt{116}$$
$$c = 10.770...$$

DE is about 10.8 units.

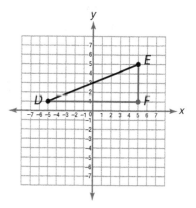

A Use a coordinate grid to find the length of a line segment.

DO

Find the length of $\overline{GH}$.

1 Add legs to form a right triangle with the given segment as the hypotenuse.

2 Label the third vertex I.

3 Count to find the lengths of GI and HI.

4 Use the Pythagorean theorem.

Length of $\overline{GI}$ = _____ units

Length of $\overline{HI}$ = _____ units

$$a^2 + b^2 = c^2$$

$$\boxed{}^2 + \boxed{}^2 = c^2$$

$$\boxed{} + \boxed{} = c^2$$

$$\boxed{} = c^2$$

$$c = \sqrt{\boxed{}}$$

$$c \approx \boxed{}$$

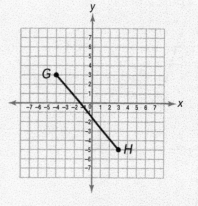

GH is about _____ units.

DISCUSS

Why is it helpful to use a coordinate grid to find the length of a segment whose endpoints have integer coordinates?

PRACTICE

Draw legs to complete each right triangle. Use the coordinate grid and the Pythagorean theorem to find the length of the hypotenuse. Round to the nearest tenth, if necessary.

1

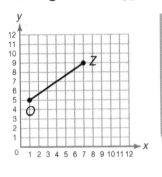

> **HINT**
> Check your work by making sure the hypotenuse is the longest side length of your triangle.

_____

2

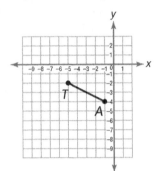

> **REMEMBER**
> Draw in the right triangle along the grid lines.

_____

3

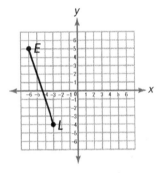

_____

4

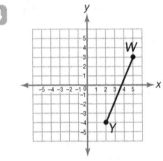

_____

5

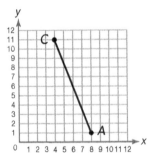

_____

6

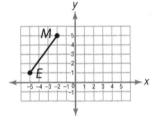

_____

7

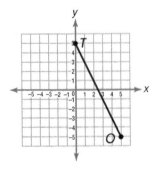

_____

8

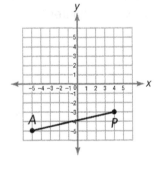

_____

Use the coordinate grid to solve.

9 An inline skating trail runs across a park from the library to city hall. A map shows their locations, with each square side representing 10 meters. How long is the trail?

Inline Skating Trail

I see! I need to know the distance that each square side represents to solve the problem.

_____

DISCUSS **Check the Reasoning**

Malik puts an X where he thinks the right angle of a right triangle belongs. He used it to solve the following question.

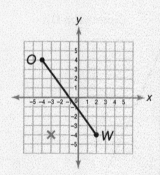

What is the length of $\overline{OW}$?

Do you agree with Malik's method? Explain.

$$a^2 + b^2 = c^2$$
$$5^2 + 8^2 = c^2$$
$$25 + 64 = c^2$$
$$89 = c^2$$
$$c = \sqrt{89}$$
$$c = 9.433...$$

OW is about 9.4 units.

PROBLEM SOLVING

DIVING

READ

The winner of a diving contest made the dive represented here. What was the length of his dive, in feet? Show the distance to one decimal place.

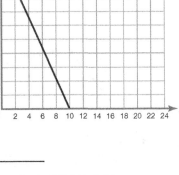

Champion Dive

PLAN

- What is the problem asking you to find?

  You need to find the _____ of the dive.

- What do you need to solve the problem?

  What does each square side represent? _____

  From what height was the dive made? _____

  How far from the end of the pool did the diver land? _____

- What method can you use?

  The coordinate grid shows a slanted line. You can use the Pythagorean theorem.

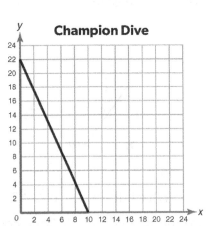

> Each square's side in the grid represents 2 feet. I need to count by 2s.

SOLVE

$$a^2 + b^2 = c^2$$

$$\underline{\quad 22 \quad}^2 + \underline{\qquad}^2 = c^2$$

$$\underline{\quad 484 \quad} + \underline{\qquad} = c^2$$

$$\underline{\qquad} = c^2$$

$$c = \sqrt{\underline{\qquad}}$$

$$c \approx \underline{\qquad\qquad}$$

The dive was about _____ feet.

Champion Dive

CHECK

Check using the Pythagorean theorem.

$$a^2 + b^2 = c^2$$

$$22^2 + 10^2 \stackrel{?}{\approx} 24.2^2$$

$$\underline{\qquad} + \underline{\qquad} \stackrel{?}{\approx} \underline{\qquad}$$

$$\underline{\qquad} \approx \underline{\qquad} \quad \checkmark$$

> I had to round my answer, so 24.2 was an approximation. And 584 ≈ 585.64. My answer checks!

The dive was about _____ feet.

PRACTICE

Use the problem-solving steps to help you. Round each answer to one decimal place.

1 Morgan climbed a tree to get a better view of a bird's nest. The coordinate grid shows his location and the location of the nest. If each square side represents 2 feet, how far away is the nest?

CHECKLIST
- [ ] READ
- [ ] PLAN
- [ ] SOLVE
- [ ] CHECK

2 The coordinate grid shows the pool at Joseph's school. A stripe is painted from one corner of the pool to the opposite corner. If each square edge represents 2 meters, how long is the stripe?

CHECKLIST
- [ ] READ
- [ ] PLAN
- [ ] SOLVE
- [ ] CHECK

3 The coordinate grid shows the side of a steep cliff that extends into a lake. If each square edge represents 1 meter, how long is the cliff?

CHECKLIST
- [ ] READ
- [ ] PLAN
- [ ] SOLVE
- [ ] CHECK

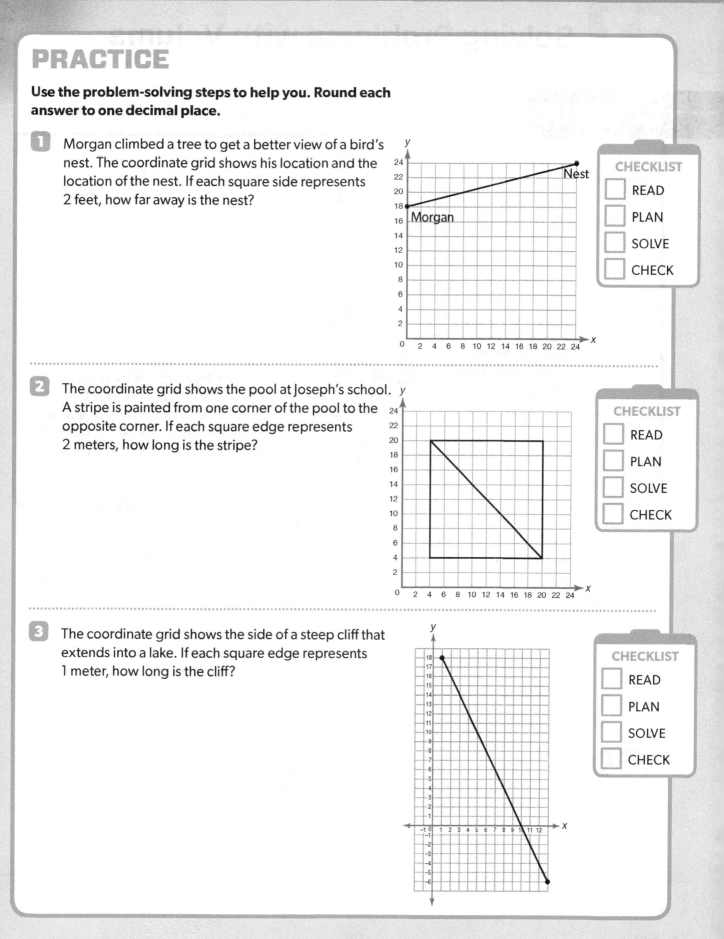

Solving Problems with Volume

PLUG IN Evaluating Algebraic Expressions

To evaluate an **algebraic expression**, use **substitution**. You can replace the variables with the given values.

Evaluate $3x^2 + \dfrac{15}{(y+1)} - 4$ for $x = 5$ and $y = 2$.

$$3 \times 5^2 + \dfrac{15}{(2+1)} - 4$$

You can evaluate the resulting **arithmetic expression** using the **order of operations**.

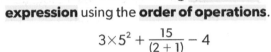

$$3 \times 5^2 + \dfrac{15}{(2+1)} - 4$$

$$3 \times 5^2 + \dfrac{15}{3} - 4$$

$$3 \times 25 + \dfrac{15}{3} - 4$$

$$75 + 5 - 4$$

$$80 - 4$$

$$76$$

I see! To substitute here, I replace the x with 5 and the y with 2.

To follow the order of operations, I first simplify within parentheses. Then I simplify exponents. Then I perform multiplication and division, from left to right. Finally I perform addition and subtraction, from left to right.

Words to Know

algebraic expression	**substitution**	**arithmetic expression**	**order of operations**
a combination of numbers and/or variables joined by operations	the replacement of a variable with a numeric value	a combination of operations and numbers	rules for simplifying expressions with multiple operations
$x^2 - 5x + 3$	$x^2 - 5x + 3$, for $x = 9$	$6^2 - 5 \times 6 + 3$	$6^2 - 5 \times 6 + (2 + 1)$
	$9^2 - 5(9) + 3$		$6^2 - 5 \times 6 + 3$
			$36 - 5 \times 6 + 3$
			$36 - 30 + 3$
			$6 + 3$
			9

 Dennis wants to evaluate $3x + 2x$ for $x = 4$. He asks if he should simplify the variable expressions to $5x$ before substituting, or if he should substitute first and then simplify. What would you tell him?

A You can evaluate an algebraic expression containing parentheses for given values.

 DO Evaluate $(2ab)^2 - 5a^2$, for $a = 3$ and $b = 2$.

① Substitute the given values for the variables.

② Simplify inside the parentheses.

③ Simplify the exponents.

④ Multiply.

⑤ Subtract.

$(2 \times \underline{\hspace{1cm}} \times \underline{\hspace{1cm}})^2 - 5 \times \underline{\hspace{1cm}}^2$

$\underline{\hspace{1cm}}^2 - 5 \times \underline{\hspace{1cm}}^2$

$\underline{\hspace{1cm}} - 5 \times \underline{\hspace{1cm}}$

$\underline{\hspace{1cm}} - \underline{\hspace{1cm}}$

$\underline{\hspace{1cm}}$

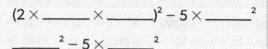 *I see! I need to multiply inside the parentheses to find the value to square.*

B You can evaluate an algebraic expression containing exponents for given values.

 DO Evaluate $4p^2q - 2p^3 \div p^2$, for $p = 3$ and $q = 5$

① Substitute the given values for the variables.

② Simplify the exponents.

③ Multiply and divide.

④ Subtract.

$4(\underline{\hspace{1cm}}^2)(\underline{\hspace{1cm}}) - 2(\underline{\hspace{1cm}}^3) \div \underline{\hspace{1cm}}^2$

$4(\underline{\hspace{1cm}})(\underline{\hspace{1cm}}) - 2(\underline{\hspace{1cm}}) \div \underline{\hspace{1cm}}$

$\underline{\hspace{1cm}} - \underline{\hspace{1cm}} \div \underline{\hspace{1cm}}$

$\underline{\hspace{1cm}} - \underline{\hspace{1cm}}$

$\underline{\hspace{1cm}}$

DISCUSS Erma knows to simplify in parentheses first, but she's not sure how to do this when the parentheses contain multiple operations. She wants to find $3 + (2 \times 5^2 - 1)$. In what order should she simplify the operations within the parentheses?

PRACTICE

Evaluate the algebraic expressions for the given values of the variables.

1 x^2; $x = 4$

$\underline{\hspace{1.5cm}}$

2 $6a^2$; $a = 2$

$\underline{\hspace{1.5cm}}$

3 $6p^2 \div q$; $p = 5$, $q = 2$

$\underline{\hspace{1.5cm}}$

4 $2m^2 + 3^2n$; $m = 2$, $n = 8$

$\underline{\hspace{1.5cm}}$

5 $8s^2 - t^3$; $s = 2$, $t = 3$

$\underline{\hspace{1.5cm}}$

6 $3z^3 - 2y^2z$; $y = 2$, $z = 4$

$\underline{\hspace{1.5cm}}$

Volume Formulas

Volume is the amount of space a three-dimensional figure takes up. Volume is measured in **cubic units**. You can use formulas to find volume.

Cones and cylinders have circular bases. The formulas for their volumes include the formula for the area of a circle.

A sphere is another three-dimensional figure based on a circle. The distance from the surface of a sphere to its center is always the same.

Cylinder

$r = 3$ in.

$h = 6$ in.

$V = \pi r^2 h$

Cone

$d = 14$ m

$h = 12$ m

$V = \frac{1}{3}\pi r^2 h$

Sphere

$r = 6$ mm

$V = \frac{4}{3}\pi r^3$

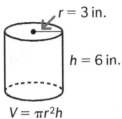

I can substitute values for variables to find volume.

I see! The volume of a cone is one-third the volume of a cylinder!

The formula for the volume of a sphere is based on just one measure: its radius!

Words to Know

volume
the amount of space taken up by a three-dimensional figure

cubic unit
a unit used to measure volume

DISCUSS Mitul makes a cone and cylinder out of construction paper. Each figure has the same height and the same radius. Which will have greater volume based on its appearance? How do their formulas confirm this to be true?

A You can use a formula to determine the volume of a cylinder.

DO Find the volume of a cylinder with a radius of 10 inches and a height of 12 inches. Use 3.14 for π.

1 Write the formula for the volume of a cylinder.

$V = \underline{\hspace{1cm}}$

2 Substitute the given value for each variable and π.

$V \approx 3.14 \times \underline{\hspace{1cm}}^2 \times \underline{\hspace{1cm}}$

$\approx 3.14 \times \underline{\hspace{1cm}} \times 12$

3 Use the order of operations to solve for V.

$\approx \underline{\hspace{1cm}}$ in.^{3}

Volume Formulas can be found on p.223.

Two common approximations for π are $\frac{22}{7}$ and 3.14.

B You can use a formula to determine the volume of a cone.

Find the volume of a cone with a diameter of 4 feet and a height of 6 feet. Use 3.14 for π.

1. Write the formula for the volume of a cone.

$V = $ _____

2. Find the value of the radius.

The radius is half the diameter: $r = \frac{1}{2}d = \frac{1}{2}(4) = $ _____ ft

3. Substitute the given value for each variable.

$V \approx \frac{1}{3} \times$ _____ $\times$ _____$^2 \times$ _____

$\approx$ _____ cubic feet

4. Use the order of operations to solve for V.

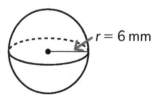

C You can use a formula to determine the volume of a sphere.

Find the volume of a sphere with a radius of 21 centimeters. Use $\frac{22}{7}$ for π.

1. Write the formula for the volume of a sphere.

$V = $ _____

2. Substitute the given value for the variable and π.

$V \approx \frac{4}{3} \times$ _____ $\times$ _____^{3}

$\approx \frac{4}{3} \times$ _____ $\times$ _____

$\approx$ _____ cubic centimeters

3. Use the order of operations to solve for V.

DISCUSS Harry knows he could use either $\frac{22}{7}$ or 3.14 for π. How would you explain why $\frac{22}{7}$ is a useful approximation for this problem?

PRACTICE

Use the formula to find the volume of each solid figure. Use either $\frac{22}{7}$ or 3.14 as an approximation for π.

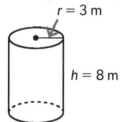

1
$r = 3$ m
$h = 8$ m

_____

2
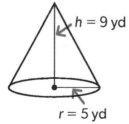
$h = 9$ yd
$r = 5$ yd

_____

3
$r = 6$ mm

_____

Solving Problems with Volume

Different three-dimensional figures have different formulas used to find their volumes.

I know the volume formulas for cones, cylinders, and spheres. And I remember the formula for the volume of a rectangular prism: $V = lwh$.

Many three-dimensional figures in the real world are combinations of these shapes. In those cases, the total volume is equal to the sum of the volumes of the individual parts.

This paper towel holder is made up of two cylinders. Each cylinder has a different radius and height.

DISCUSS What is the shape of a rectangular solid whose length, width, and height are all equal? What happens to the formula for its volume?

LESSON LINK

PLUG IN	POWER UP	GO!

You can evaluate algebraic expressions using substitution.

Evaluate

$x^2 + 3x + 5$ for $x = 4$

$4^2 + 3 \times 4 + 5$

$16 + 12 + 5$

$28 + 5$

33

You can find the volume of three-dimensional objects using formulas.

$V = lwh$

$V = \pi r^2 h$

$V = \frac{1}{3} \pi r^2 h$

$V = \frac{4}{3} \pi r^3$

I get it! I can use formulas to solve problems involving volume.

WORK TOGETHER

Find the volume of this ice cream treat.

- The volume of the cone is 616 cubic centimeters.

- The volume of the half-sphere is $718\frac{2}{3}$ cubic centimeters.

- The total volume is $1{,}334\frac{2}{3}$ cubic centimeters.

- This is a cone with a hemisphere (a half-sphere) on top.

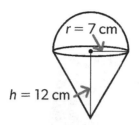

$r = 7$ cm

$h = 12$ cm

Volume Formulas can be found on p. 223.

cone:

$$V = \frac{1}{3}\pi r^2 h$$

$$V \approx \frac{1}{3} \times \frac{22}{7} \times 7^2 \times 12$$

$$\approx \frac{1}{3} \times \frac{22}{7} \times 49 \times 12$$

$$\approx 616 \text{ cm}^3$$

hemisphere:

$$V = \frac{1}{2} \times \frac{4}{3}\pi r^3$$

$$V \approx \frac{1}{2} \times \frac{4}{3} \times \frac{22}{7} \times 7^3$$

$$\approx \frac{1}{2} \times \frac{4}{3} \times \frac{22}{7} \times 343$$

$$\approx 718\frac{2}{3} \text{ cm}^3$$

Total $V \approx 616 + 718\frac{2}{3} \approx 1{,}334\frac{2}{3}$ cm^3

A You can use multiple formulas to find the volume of a three-dimensional figure. Use 3.14 for π.

DO Find the volume.

❶ Write the volume formulas for a cone and a cylinder.

❷ Substitute the given values for the variables.

❸ Find the volume of each object.

❹ Add to find the total volume.

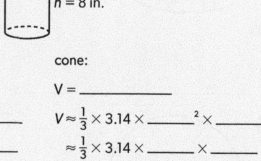

$h = 10$ in.

$r = 3$ in.

$h = 8$ in.

cylinder:

$V = $ _____

$V \approx 3.14 \times$ _____$^2 \times$ _____

$\approx 3.14 \times$ _____ $\times$ _____

$\approx$ _____

cone:

$V = $ _____

$V \approx \frac{1}{3} \times 3.14 \times$ _____$^2 \times$ _____

$\approx \frac{1}{3} \times 3.14 \times$ _____ $\times$ _____

$\approx$ _____

Total $V \approx$ _____ $+$ _____ $\approx$ _____ in.^{3}

DISCUSS If a figure was made of three cones of the same height and radius, what would its formula be? What formula would it be equal to?

PRACTICE

Find the volume. Use either 3.14 or $\frac{22}{7}$ for π.

1

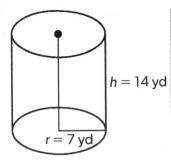

$h = 14$ yd

$r = 7$ yd

> **REMEMBER**
> Diagrams may show diameters of figures, but the volume formulas use the radius.

2

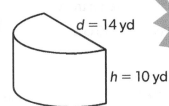

$d = 14$ yd

$h = 10$ yd

> **Volume Formulas** can be found on pp. 223 and 227

_____

_____

3

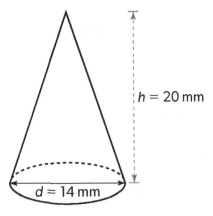

$h = 20$ mm

$d = 14$ mm

4

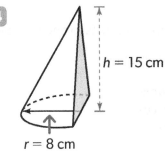

$h = 15$ cm

$r = 8$ cm

_____

_____

5

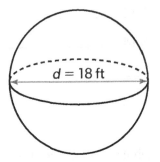

$d = 18$ ft

6

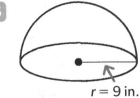

$r = 9$ in.

_____

_____

Find the volume. Use $\frac{22}{7}$ or 3.14 for π.

7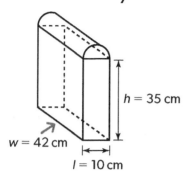

$h = 35$ cm

$w = 42$ cm

$l = 10$ cm

8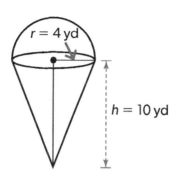

$r = 4$ yd

$h = 10$ yd

9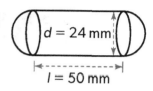

$d = 24$ mm

$l = 50$ mm

_____

_____ _____

Find the volume of the described object. Use $\frac{22}{7}$ or 3.14 for π.

10 Half a of a cone with a diameter 11 inches and a height of 4 inches

_____

11 Half of a cylinder with a radius of 15 millimeters and a height of 40 millimeters

_____

HINT
Use the formulas to find the volume of the whole figure and then divide the volume by 2.

 Study the Pattern!

Marta wrote the volume formulas for a sphere, a cylinder, and a cone.

Sphere
$V = \frac{4}{3}\pi r^3$

Cylinder
$V = \pi r^2 h$

Cone
$V = \frac{1}{3}\pi r^2 h$

If a cylinder has a height equal to its radius, how would the volume of the cylinder compare to the volume of a sphere with the same radius? How would its volume compare to a cone with the same radius? Explain.

PROBLEM SOLVING

HAY! IT'S A BARN!

READ

The bottom section of a barn is a rectangular prism. The top section of the roof is half a cylinder. What is the volume of the barn? Use 3.14 for π.

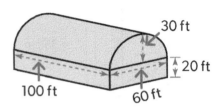

30 ft

20 ft

100 ft

60 ft

PLAN

• What is the problem asking you to find?

the _____ of the barn

• How can you solve this problem?

Find the _____ of each figure and then _____ the volumes together.

• Which formulas will you use?

rectangular prism: _____ half cylinder: _____

SOLVE

Find the volume of the rectangular prism. $V = $ **100** $\times$ **60** $\times$ _____ $=$ _____ ft^3

Find the volume of the half cylinder. $V \approx \frac{1}{2} \times$ _____ $\times$ _____ $\times$ _____

$\approx \frac{1}{2} \times$ _____ $\times$ _____ $\times$ _____ $\approx \frac{1}{2} \times$ _____ ft^3 $=$ _____ ft^3

Add the volumes of the two figures. _____ $+$ _____ $=$ _____ ft^3

CHECK

Use $\frac{22}{7}$ for π in the formula for a half cylinder.

$V = \approx \frac{1}{2} \times \frac{22}{7} \times$ _____ $\times$ _____

$\approx$ _____ ft^3

The volume of the rectangular solid will not change.

$V = $ _____

Add to find the total volume. _____ $+$ _____

$= $ _____ ft^3

Compare the two solutions to see if they are close.

_____

_____

The volume of the barn is about _____.

PRACTICE

Use the problem-solving steps to help you.

1 The shape of a greenhouse is close to the shape of half of a sphere with a diameter of 26 ft. What is the approximate volume of the greenhouse? Use $\frac{22}{7}$ for π.

CHECKLIST
- [ ] READ
- [ ] PLAN
- [ ] SOLVE
- [ ] CHECK

2 A chute at a factory drops cereal into boxes. What is the maximum volume of the chute? Use 3.14 for π.

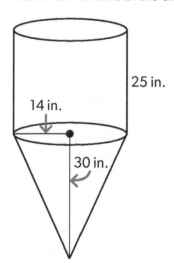

25 in.

14 in.

30 in.

CHECKLIST
- [ ] READ
- [ ] PLAN
- [ ] SOLVE
- [ ] CHECK

3 A machine part consists of a steel plate with a hole in the center. What is the volume of the steel plate? Use 3.14 for π.

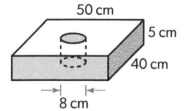

50 cm

5 cm

40 cm

8 cm

CHECKLIST
- [ ] READ
- [ ] PLAN
- [ ] SOLVE
- [ ] CHECK

PLUG IN Identifying Association in a Scatter Plot

You can look at how the data points are clustered in this **scatter plot** to determine if there is a relationship between outside temperature and ice cream sales.

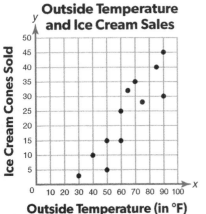

Outside Temperature and Ice Cream Sales

Ice Cream Cones Sold (y-axis)
Outside Temperature (in °F) (x-axis)

Decide if the data points cluster in a straight line or a curve, or if they look randomly scattered. Then you can identify the **association** between the sets of data.

- **Linear association:** The data resembles a straight line. You can also describe a linear association as positive or negative, depending on the slope of the line.

- **Nonlinear association:** The data resembles a curve.

- **No association:** The data is randomly scattered.

In this scatter plot, the x-coordinate in each ordered pair represents the temperature and the y-coordinate represents ice cream sales.

I see! The data in this scatter plot shows a positive linear association because the points cluster together like a line with a positive slope.

Words to Know

scatter plot	association	linear association	nonlinear association
a graph of ordered pairs that shows the relationship between two sets of data	the relationship between data points on a scatter plot	a relationship shown on a scatter plot in which data points resemble a straight line	a relationship shown on a scatter plot in which data points resemble a curve

DISCUSS

Maja sees a scatter plot in which each point lies along a horizontal line. She says the line that the points would cluster around has zero slope, so the scatter plot shows no association. Is she correct? Explain why or why not.

A You can look at how data points are clustered to describe an association.

> The association describes the relationship between the two variables graphed on a scatter plot.

DO What is the association, if any, between sleep and test scores?

1. Determine how the data points cluster.

2. Determine whether the association is positive or negative.

3. Make a statement about the association.

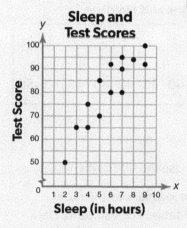

Sleep and Test Scores

The data points cluster in a _____ so there is a _____ association.

Because the data points cluster upwards from left to right, the association is _____.

This scatter plot shows a _____ _____ association between sleep and test scores.

DISCUSS How does the description of a linear association relate to slope?

PRACTICE

Write "linear association," "nonlinear association," or "no association" for each scatter plot.

 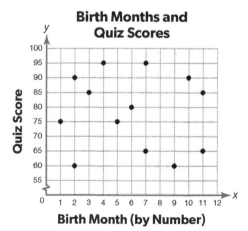

Birth Months and Quiz Scores

_____

2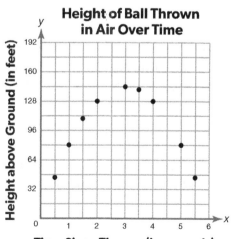

Height of Ball Thrown in Air Over Time

_____

Constructing Scatter Plots

You can construct a scatter plot using data in a table.

Children's Ages and Heights

Age (in years)	1	2	3	3	4	4	5	7	8	9
Height (in inches)	25	30	35	40	35	40	40	45	45	50

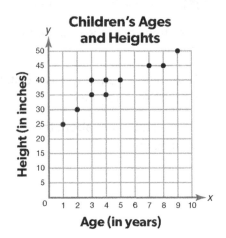

1. **Title the scatter plot**. Use the title of the table.

2. **Label and number the x-axis**. Use the label from the top row of the table. The values for data in that row range from 1 to 9. A good **scale** to use is 0 to 10, with intervals of 1.

3. **Label and number the y-axis**. Use the label from the bottom row of the table. The values for that variable range from 25 to 50. A good scale to use is 0 to 50, with intervals of 5.

4. **Plot a point for each ordered pair**. Plot points at (1, 25), (2, 30), (3, 35), (3, 40), and so on.

> I get it! I have to choose a scale that lets me fit all the data points I have on the scatter plot.

Words to Know

x-axis	scale	y-axis
the horizontal number line on an *x-y* coordinate graph	numbers that change at regular intervals along an axis of a graph	the vertical number line on an *x-y* coordinate graph

DISCUSS

Devon is planning a scatter plot for the data points (1, 5), (5, 45), (9, 28). He decides to make the scale for each axis 0 to 50. Would you agree or disagree with his choice? Explain.

A You can construct a scatter plot to show the data in a table.

Choosing the right scale for each axis lets me see all of the data clearly.

DO

Construct a scatter plot to show these data.

DVD Sales and Release Dates

Weeks Since Release	0	1	1	2	3	3	4	4	5
Number Sold	18	16	14	12	13	10	12	8	9

① Label the *x*-axis using the name of the variable in the first row. Choose a scale.

For the *x*-axis, use a scale of _____ to _____, with intervals of $\frac{1}{2}$.

② Label the *y*-axis using the name of the variable in the second row. Choose a scale.

For the *y*-axis, use a scale of 0 to _____, with intervals of 2.

③ Plot each ordered pair in the table as a point.

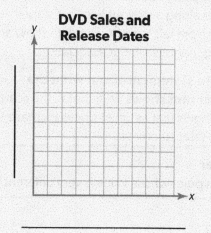

DVD Sales and Release Dates

PRACTICE

Construct a scatter plot to show the data in the table. Include a title, scales, and axis labels.

Rainfall and Umbrella Sales

Rainfall (in inches)	0	1	1	2	2	3	4	4
Number Sold	1	2	3	3	5	6	8	9

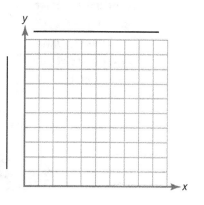

Temperature and Scarf Sales

Temperature (in °F)	20	30	30	40	50	50	60	80
Number Sold	18	16	12	10	7	4	5	2

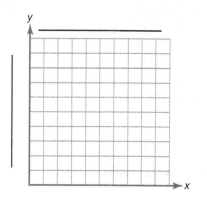

You can use a scatter plot to determine if (and how) data pairs are related. This scatter plot shows data for concert ticket prices and the number of tickets sold.

I get it! A scatter plot lets me see an association in data and then explain what it means.

1 **Identify any outliers**. The point at (80, 450) is an outlier because it is very different from all of the other points. Do not consider the outlier when looking for an association.

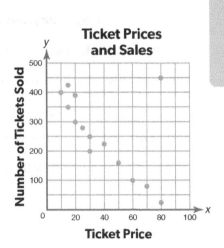

Ticket Prices and Sales

Number of Tickets Sold vs Ticket Price

2 **Identify any association**. The points cluster along a straight line that slopes down from left to right. The data show a strong, negative linear association.

3 **Make a statement about what the scatter plot shows**. In general, the scatter plot shows that as ticket prices increase, ticket sales decrease.

Words to Know

outlier
a data point whose value is very different from other data points on a scatter plot

DISCUSS Andre isn't sure why he would want to consider a data value an outlier. What would you tell him?

LESSON LINK

PLUG IN	POWER UP	GO!

You can look at how data points are clustered to find an association.

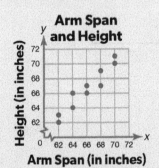

Arm Span and Height

Height (in inches) vs Arm Span (in inches)

positive linear association

You can construct a scatter plot to show ordered pairs of data.

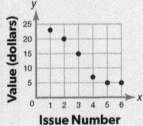

Comic Book Value by Issue Number

Value (dollars) vs Issue Number

I get it! I can construct a scatter plot and make a statement about how the pairs of data are related.

WORK TOGETHER

You can interpret a scatter plot.

An English teacher made this scatter plot to show the number of pages he assigns and how many days it takes his students to finish reading these pages.

- Identify any outliers.

- Identify any association among the other points.

- Make a statement about what the scatter plot shows.

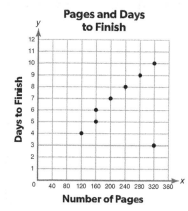

Pages and Days to Finish

Days to Finish (y) vs *Number of Pages* (x)

The outlier is at (320, 3).

The data show a positive, linear association.

The more pages he assigns, the longer it takes his students to finish reading them.

A You can construct a scatter plot to see if pairs of data are related.

DO

The table shows the ages, in months, of used computers and their selling prices.

Age (in months)	6	12	12	18	24	24	30	36	36	48
Selling Price (in $)	400	450	400	300	250	150	200	450	100	50

1 Construct a scatter plot.

2 Identify any outliers.

3 Describe the association, if any, shown.

4 Describe what the scatter plot shows.

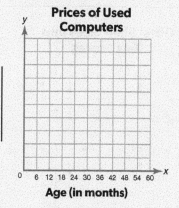

Prices of Used Computers

Age (in months)

The outlier is at (36, _____).

The data shows a _____ linear association.

It shows that the older a computer is, the

_____.

DISCUSS

Josh records the heights and weights of his football teammates. He makes a scatter plot and determines that there is a weak, positive association between height and weight. Describe how his scatter plot must look.

PRACTICE

Describe any association shown. Identify any outliers. Then explain, in general, what the scatter plot shows.

1

Practice Time and Band Grades

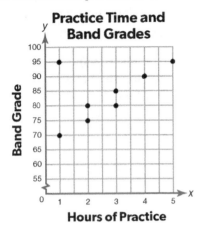

There is a _____ _____ association.

outlier(s): _____

In general, the longer students' practice

times, _____.

2

Prices and Number Ordered

There is a _____ _____ association.

outlier(s): _____

In general, the more boxes ordered, the

_____.

3

Girls' Shoe Sizes and Test Scores

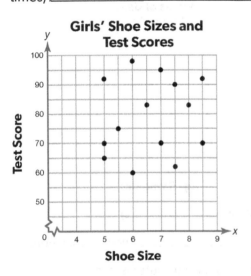

There is _____ association.

outlier(s): _____

In general, _____

_____.

4

Fathers' and Sons' Heights

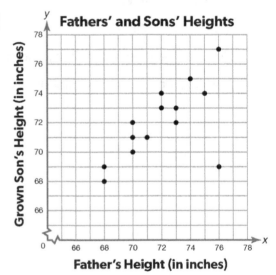

There is a _____ _____ association.

outlier(s): _____

In general, _____

_____.

Construct a scatter plot. Identify any outliers. Describe and interpret any association between the data points.

5 The table shows the prices of bowls of soup and the number of bowls sold.

Prices and Soup Sales

Price of Soup (in $)	2	3	3	4	4	5	5	6	7	8
Number Sold	36	28	32	24	20	16	10	8	4	32

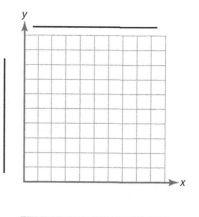

Outlier(s): _____

_____

_____

_____

Critiquing Others' Reasoning

The scatter plot shows English grades and math grades for each student in Karim's homeroom. Karim says one student earned a 65 in English and a 95 in math, so there is no association between the English grades and math grades. What can you tell Karim about his reasoning?

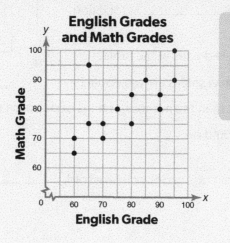

English Grades and Math Grades

> When looking for an association, I have to look at the general relationship of the data points.

PROBLEM SOLVING

HOW CORNY

READ

The owner of a movie theater recorded data to see if there was an association between popcorn sales and drink sales. What association, if any, does the data show?

Popcorn and Drink Sales

Bags of Popcorn Sold	40	60	80	100	100	120	140	140	160
Drinks Sold	140	60	90	110	140	120	160	180	180

PLAN

• What does the problem ask you to find out?

if there is an association between _____ and _____

• What do you need to do to solve the problem?

Construct a _____. Determine if the data points cluster along

_____.

SOLVE

On the grid, construct a scatter plot.

The point at (___40___, _____) is an outlier.

The other data points slope _____ from left to right.

Except for the outlier, the data show a

_____, _____ association.

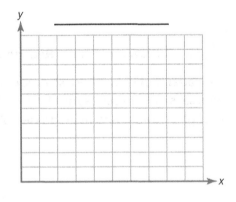

CHECK

Compare the ordered pairs in the table.

The number of drinks sold is always equal to _____

or _____ than the number of bags of popcorn sold. So it makes sense that

the association would be _____.

In general, as more bags of popcorn are sold, _____.

PRACTICE

Use the problem-solving steps to help you.

1 Janina collected data for how much she and her sisters used their exercise bike. In the scatter plot, she recorded how many hours each person used it and the number of months since they bought It. Based on the data, is there an association between the number of months since the bike was purchased and the number of hours it was used each month? Use the scatter plot to support your answer.

CHECKLIST

☐ READ
☐ PLAN
☐ SOLVE
☐ CHECK

Sisters' Use of Exercise Bike

2 Rachel wonders how science test scores are associated with the amount of time students are given to complete these tests. The table compares the number of minutes that students were given to complete a science test and their scores on the test. Make a scatter plot and interpret the data.

CHECKLIST

☐ READ
☐ PLAN
☐ SOLVE
☐ CHECK

Time Spent and Test Scores

Minutes Given to Complete Test	15	20	20	25	30	35	40	45	45
Test Score	75	60	95	90	75	65	90	60	80

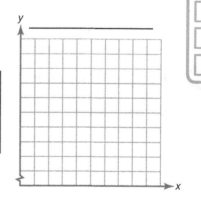

Solving Problems with Scatter Plots

PLUG IN · Identifying a Trend Line

A **trend line** is a straight line that shows how data points cluster on a scatter plot. A trend line can show a positive linear **association**.

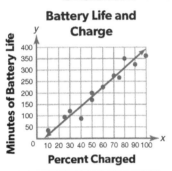

Battery Life and Charge

y-axis: Minutes of Battery Life
x-axis: Percent Charged

Or a trend line can show a negative linear association.

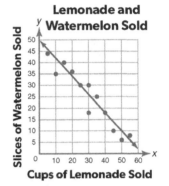

Lemonade and Watermelon Sold

y-axis: Slices of Watermelon Sold
x-axis: Cups of Lemonade Sold

> A trend line is also called the line of best fit. The trend line shown has a positive slope because the trend in the data is that as *x* increases, *y* increases.

> The trend in these data is that as *x* increases, *y* decreases. That means the trend line has a negative slope.

Words to Know

trend line
a straight line that best shows the linear relationship between data points on a scatter plot

association
the relationship between data points on a scatter plot

DISCUSS Would it be useful to draw a trend line for a scatter plot that shows a nonlinear association? Explain.

A You can determine the association represented by a trend line.

DO Describe the association shown by the trend line.

1. Look at the pattern of the data points.

2. Check the sign of the slope of the trend line.

3. Describe the association shown by the trend line.

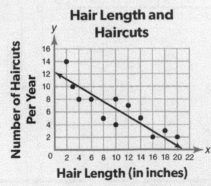

Hair Length and Haircuts

y-axis: Number of Haircuts Per Year
x-axis: Hair Length (in inches)

The trend is that as *x* increases,

y _____.

The slope is _____.

The trend line shows a

_____ linear association.

B You can use the association represented by a trend line to predict data points.

The data set shows the number of guests staying at new hotels and the number of months these hotels have been open. Based on the trend line, would you expect the number of guests at a new hotel in month 7 to be greater or less than its number of guests in month 6?

1 Look at the pattern of the data points.

2 Check the sign of the slope of the trend line.

3 Describe the association shown by the trend line.

4 Answer the question based on the association shown.

Guests Staying at New Hotels

Number of Guests

Months after Opening

The trend is that as x increases,

y _____.

The slope is _____.

The trend line shows a

_____ linear association.

The number of guests

_____ with every additional month the hotel is open. So the number of guests at a new hotel in month 7 should

be _____ than the number of guests in month 6.

DISCUSS Would you be able to predict data points for a data set that showed no association? Explain.

PRACTICE

Describe the association represented by the trend line.

1

Length of Chalk after Class Use

Length of Chalk (in inches)

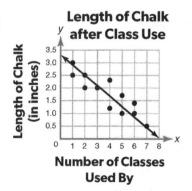

Number of Classes Used By

The trend line shows a _____ linear association.

Use the association represented by the trend line to predict data points.

2

Birds Seen at Bird Feeders

Number of Birds Seen Per Day

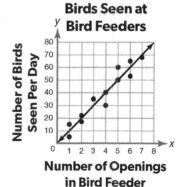

Number of Openings in Bird Feeder

Based on the trend line, is the number of birds at a bird feeder with 6 openings greater or less than at a feeder with

5 openings? _____

185

POWER UP — Drawing a Trend Line

A trend line follows the general association between the data points.

Number of Sandwiches in an Office Vending Machine

Data points do not have to fall on the trend line.

> A trend line rarely fits every point exactly. Instead, it represents the general trend of the entire data set.

Do not consider **outliers** when drawing a trend line.

Number of Sandwiches in an Office Vending Machine

> Since the trend line should show the main trend of the data points, I won't consider outliers when I draw it.

Draw a trend line that has about the same number of points above it as below it.

Number of Sandwiches in an Office Vending Machine

> I see! The trend line is a good fit if it passes through the middle of the data points.

Words to Know

outlier
a data point whose value is very different from other data points on a scatter plot

DISCUSS Could you draw more than one possible trend line for a scatter plot?

A You can draw a trend line for a scatter plot.

DO Draw a trend line for this graph of the number of cookies eaten after meals based on the number of hours since the last meal.

1. Identify outliers of the data set.

2. Describe the association between the data points.

3. Identify the sign of the slope of the trend line.

4. Draw a line that best fits the data points.

Cookies Eaten after Meals

There is an outlier at (____, ____). Do not consider this point when drawing the trend line.

The linear association is

_____.

The slope will be _____.

186 LESSON 19

DISCUSS Tamiko drew this trend line on the scatter plot. What can you tell her about her work?

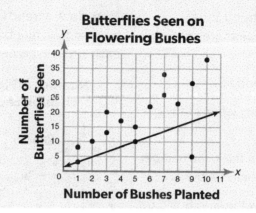

Butterflies Seen on Flowering Bushes

Number of Butterflies Seen / *Number of Bushes Planted*

PRACTICE

Draw a trend line for each scatter plot.

1 Temperature of Food in Freezer

Temperature of Food (in °F) / Time in Freezer (in minutes)

2 Snow Shovel Sales and Snowfall

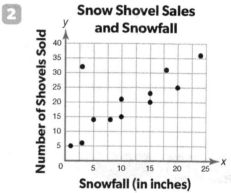

Number of Shovels Sold / Snowfall (in inches)

3 Dinosaur Body Length and Tooth Length

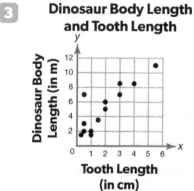

Dinosaur Body Length (in m) / Tooth Length (in cm)

4 Effects of Coffee Drinking on Sleep

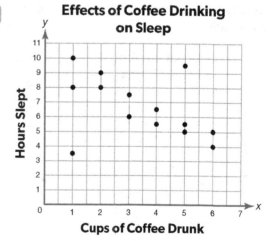

Hours Slept / Cups of Coffee Drunk

You can judge the fit of a trend line by looking at how the data points are spaced around the line.

For a trend line to be a good fit:

1 Do not consider outliers when judging the line of best fit.

2 There should be about the same number of points above the line as below it.

3 The data points below the line should be about the same distances from the line as the data points above it.

So this trend line is a good fit.

Mark drew a trend line on a scatter plot of the relationship between the number of owls and pigeons spotted on each street in his neighborhood.

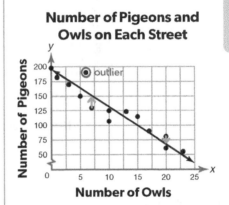

Number of Pigeons and Owls on Each Street

After drawing a trend line, I need to check if it is a good fit!

DISCUSS

In the graph above, how does the distance to the line from the farthest point below the line compare to the distance to the line from farthest non-outlier point above it? What does that tell you about the trend line?

LESSON LINK

PLUG IN	**POWER UP**	**GO!**

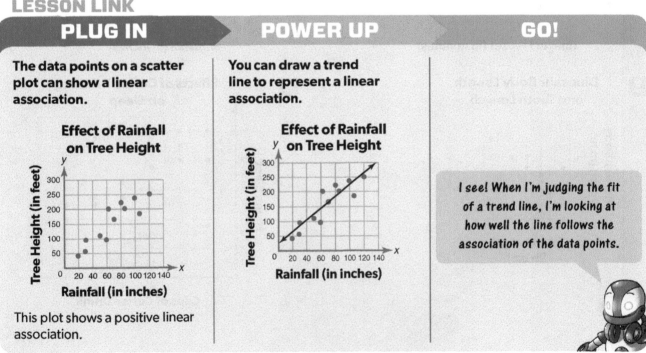

The data points on a scatter plot can show a linear association.

Effect of Rainfall on Tree Height

This plot shows a positive linear association.

You can draw a trend line to represent a linear association.

Effect of Rainfall on Tree Height

I see! When I'm judging the fit of a trend line, I'm looking at how well the line follows the association of the data points.

WORK TOGETHER

You can evaluate the fit of a trend line.

- Do not consider the outlier(s).

- Compare the number of points above and below the line.

- Compare the distances of points above and below the line.

- Evaluate the fit.

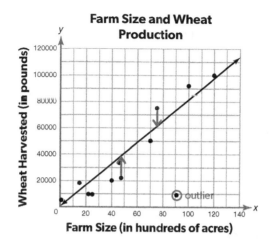

Farm Size and Wheat Production

There are about the same number of points above the line as below it. The points above the line are about the same distances from the line as the ones below it. So this line is a good fit.

A You may be able to redraw a trend line for a better fit.

DO Draw a new trend line that fits the data set better.

1. Compare the number of points above and below the line.

2. Evaluate where to draw the new line for a better fit.

3. Count the number of points above and below the proposed new line.

4. Draw a new trend line.

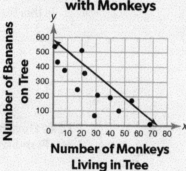

Bananas Remaining on Trees with Monkeys

Are there more points above or below the trend line?

_____

Roughly, how many points will be above the new trend line? _____

Roughly, how many points will be below the new trend line? _____

Should you draw a new trend line to pass through more of the lower or higher points? _____

DISCUSS Explain how to evaluate the trend line of the scatter plot. Then draw a new trend line for better fit.

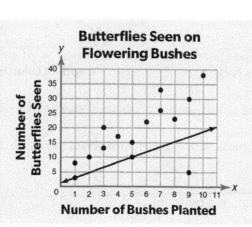

Butterflies Seen on Flowering Bushes

PRACTICE

Evaluate the fit of the trend line.

1

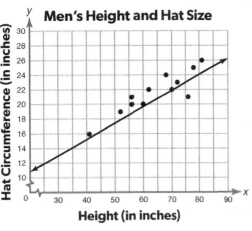

Men's Height and Hat Size

Are there about the same number of points above the line as below it? _____

Are the points above the line about the same distances from the line as the ones below it?

_____

Is this trend line a good fit for the data?

_____

> **REMEMBER**
> Don't consider outliers when evaluating the fit of a trend line.

2

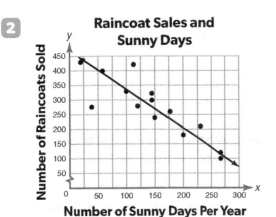

Raincoat Sales and Sunny Days

Are there about the same number of points above the line as below it? _____

Are the points above the line about the same distances from the line as the ones below it?

_____

Is this trend line a good fit for the data?

_____

3

A

Lake Depth and Fish Size

B

Lake Depth and Fish Size

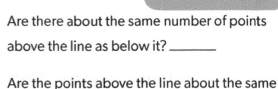

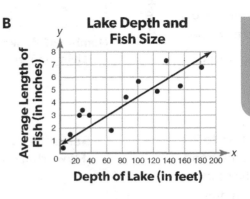

> **HINT**
> The answers for all three of the blanks below should be the same.

Graph _____ has about the same number of points above and below the trend line.

In graph _____, the data points above the line are about the same distances from the line as the ones below it.

The trend line in graph _____ is a better fit.

Draw a new trend line that has a better fit.

4

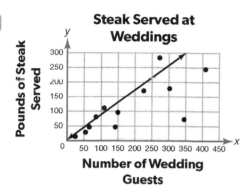

Steak Served at Weddings

5

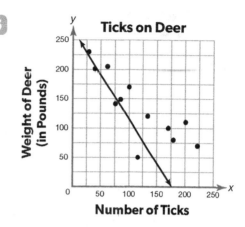

Ticks on Deer

Evaluate the fit of the trend line.

6 Bernice draws a trend line and considers the outlier as part of the data set. The trend line has 10 points above it and 5 points below. The points above the line are farther away from the line than the points below it. Explain why this trend line is or is not a good fit.

_____

_____

_____

DISCUSS

Many Possible Trend Lines

Olga and Keshawn each drew trend lines for the same scatter plot.

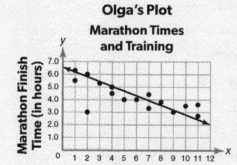

Olga's Plot

Marathon Times and Training

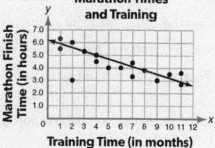

Keshawn's Plot

Marathon Times and Training

Whose trend line is a better fit for the data? Explain your answer.

PROBLEM SOLVING

WORD COUNT

READ

The scatter plot shows the number of words in different book reports. Based on the trend line for the data, would you expect a 6-page book report to have 2,200 words?

PLAN

• Find the predicted number of _____ in 6 pages.

• Find the _____ for the scatter plot.

• Read the value from the _____.

SOLVE

Identify outliers.

An outlier is at (____2____, _____).

Describe the association between the data points that are not outliers.

The data points show a _____ linear association.

Draw a line that best fits the data points.

Read the value you need from the trend line.

Based on the trend line, the predicted number of _____

for a _____-page report is _____.

Number of Words in Report

Number of Pages in Report

CHECK

Use reasoning to check your answer.

On the scatter plot, as x _____, y _____.

So the predicted number of _____ for a 6 page-report

should be _____ than for a 7-page report.

From the trend line, the predicted number of _____ for

a 7-page report is about _____.

Would you expect a 6-page report to have 2,200 words? _____

PRACTICE

Use the problem-solving steps to help you.
Solve the problem using a trend line.

1 The scatter plot shows the number of minutes used per month for different cell phone plans. Based on the trend line for the data, about how many minutes per month would you expect to be used with a plan that costs $80 per month?

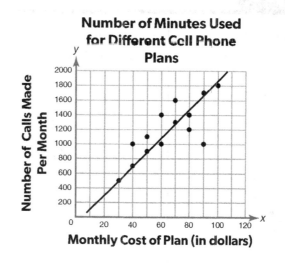

Number of Minutes Used for Different Cell Phone Plans

CHECKLIST
- ☐ READ
- ☐ PLAN
- ☐ SOLVE
- ☐ CHECK

2 The scatter plot shows the number of costumes sold on the days before Halloween. Based on the trend line for the data, about how many costumes would you expect to be sold 7 days before Halloween?

Costume Sales on the Days Before Halloween

CHECKLIST
- ☐ READ
- ☐ PLAN
- ☐ SOLVE
- ☐ CHECK

3 The scatter plot shows the number of downloads of a new song in the days after it is released. Based on the trend line for the data, about how many downloads would you expect for a new song 4 weeks after it is released?

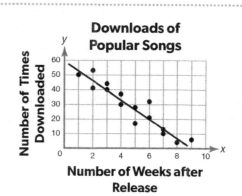

Downloads of Popular Songs

CHECKLIST
- ☐ READ
- ☐ PLAN
- ☐ SOLVE
- ☐ CHECK

A **linear model** is a line that represents a data set. The equation of a line can be written in the form $y = mx + b$.

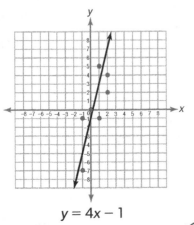

$$y = 4x - 1$$

You can read the **slope**, m, and the **y-intercept**, b, of a line from an equation in this form.

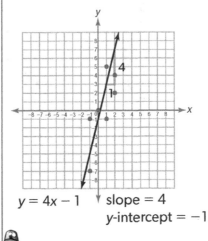

$y = 4x - 1$ slope = 4
y-intercept = −1

You can use the slope and y-intercept to write an equation for a line.

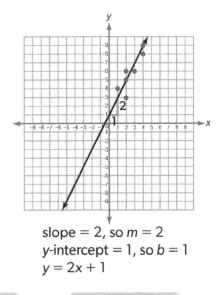

slope = 2, so $m = 2$
y-intercept = 1, so $b = 1$
$y = 2x + 1$

> I can use this form of a linear equation to model certain data sets.

> I see! A slope measures the rate of change, and the y-intercept tells me where the line crosses the y-axis.

> I get it! I can substitute these values into the linear equation $y = mx + b$.

Words to Know

linear model
a line that represents a data set, whose equation can be written in the form $y = mx + b$

slope
a ratio of the change in y-coordinates (*rise*) of a graph to the change in corresponding x-coordinates (*run*); the symbol for slope is m

y-intercept
the y-coordinate of the point at which a line crosses the y-axis

DISCUSS

Mabel says a linear model can have the equation $y = 3x + 3$. Owen says that the slope and y-intercept can't have the same value. Who is correct? Explain.

A You can find the slope of a linear model using two coordinates.

DO Find the slope of a linear model that passes through the points $(-2, 3)$ and $(1, 6)$.

1 Identify the x and y-coordinates for each point.

The x-coordinates are -2 and _____.

2 Calculate $\frac{\text{change in } y}{\text{change in } x}$ to find the slope, m.

The y-coordinates are _____ and 6.

The slope is $\dfrac{\boxed{} - \boxed{}}{\boxed{} - \boxed{}} = \dfrac{\boxed{}}{\boxed{}} = \boxed{}$

The slope is _____.

B You can find the y-intercept of a linear model using the slope and the coordinates of a point.

DO Find the y-intercept of a linear model whose slope is 3 and which contains the point $(3, 4)$.

1 Write the equation of a line.

$y = mx + b$

2 Replace the m with the value given for the slope.

_____ $= ($_____$)($_____$) + b$

3 Replace x and y with the coordinates of the point.

_____ $=$ _____ $+ b$

4 Solve for the y-intercept, b.

_____ $= b$

The y-intercept is _____.

PRACTICE

Identify the slope and y-intercept of the following linear models.

1 $y = \frac{3}{2}x - 4$

_____

2 $y = 7x + 5$

_____

Find the slope of the linear model that contains the following coordinate pairs.

3 $(-1, 2), (4, 1)$

_____

4 $(3, -1), (0, 2)$

_____

Find the y-intercept of each linear model.

5 Slope is 4 and it contains the point $(1, 1)$.

_____

6 Slope is -3 and it contains the point $(0, 0)$.

_____

Cassy drew the following linear model.

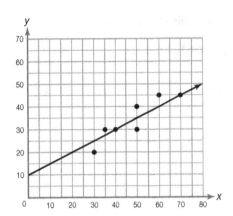

I see! I can write an equation to represent a linear model.

Write an equation that represents her linear model.

1 **Identify the y-intercept.** The y-intercept is where the line intersects with the y-axis.

The y-intercept is 10.

2 **Calculate the slope.** Find the $\frac{\text{change in } y}{\text{change in } x}$ for any pair of points on the line.

Two points on the line are $(0, 10)$ and $(40, 30)$, so

$$m = \frac{30 - 10}{40 - 0} = \frac{20}{40} \text{ or } \frac{1}{2}.$$

3 **Write the equation in slope-intercept form.** Use the form $y = mx + b$, where m represents the slope and b represents the y-intercept.

$b = 10$

$$y = \frac{1}{2}x + 10$$

The equation is $y = \frac{1}{2}x + 10$.

 Dwayne says he can't find the y-intercept of a linear model because the line passes through the origin. What would you tell him?

A You can find the slope and y-intercept of a linear model using a graph.

DO   Find the slope and y-intercept of the line. Write the equation of the line.

1 Identify the y-intercept.

2 Find the slope.

3 Write the equation of the line.

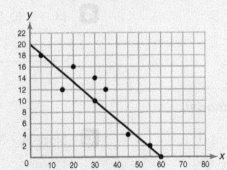

The y-intercept is _____.

Use points $(30, 10)$ and $(60, 0)$ to find the slope.

$$\frac{0 - 10}{60 - 30} = \frac{\square}{\square} = \frac{\square}{\square}$$

$y = $ _____ $x + $ _____

B You can graph a linear model for an equation written in slope-intercept form.

DO

Graph the line $y = \frac{1}{3}x + 50$ on this data set.

① Plot the y-intercept.

② Use the slope to determine another point.

③ Draw the line that passes through these two points.

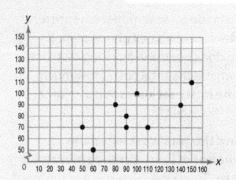

DISCUSS

Yolanda remembers that the line for a linear model should represent the trend of data points on a graph. How does the linear model in the previous problem represent the trends of the data points?

PRACTICE

Write the equation for each linear model.

1

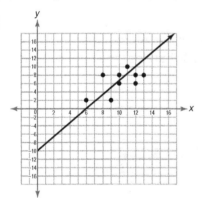

_____

2

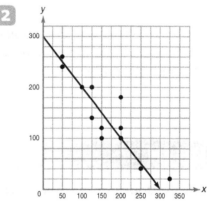

_____

Graph each linear model.

3 $y = -\frac{4}{5}x + 45$

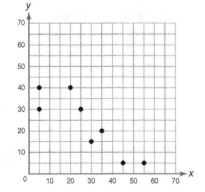

4 $y = \frac{4}{3}x + 8$

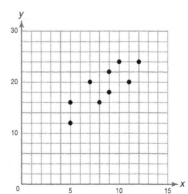

Solving Problems with Linear Equations

Darren made a linear model to represent the total cost of his cell phone plan. If Darren does not make any long distance calls, what is the total cost? How much does the total cost increase per minute of long distance?

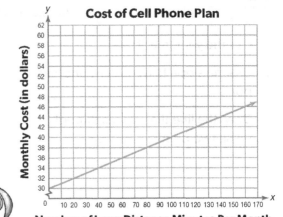

Cost of Cell Phone Plan

Monthly Cost (in dollars)

Number of Long Distance Minutes Per Month

① **Find the total cost when the number of long distance minutes is zero.** This is the y-intercept of the line. When $x = 0$, the total cost is $30.

② **Find the cost per minute of long distance.**
This is the slope of the line.

$$\frac{\text{change in } y}{\text{change in } x} = \frac{32 - 30}{20 - 0} = \frac{2}{20} = \frac{1}{10} = 0.10$$

The cost per minute of long distance is $0.10.

I see! I can solve the problem by finding the slope and y-intercept.

 DISCUSS

Tia writes the equation, $C = 0.50n + 40$, to model the cost of her internet plan. In her equation, C is the total cost when she downloads n movies. What does the rate of change of her model represent?

LESSON LINK

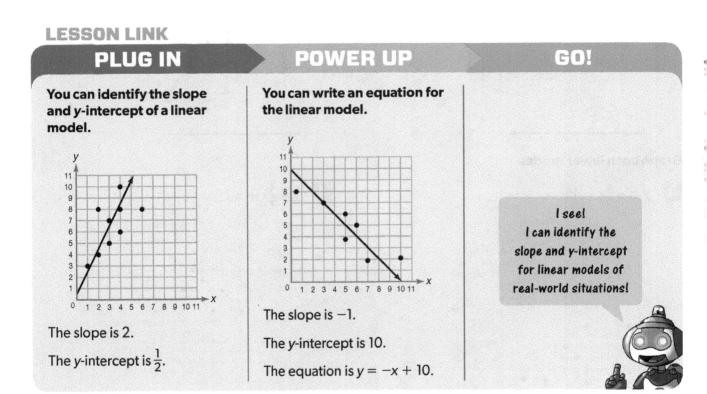

PLUG IN

You can identify the slope and y-intercept of a linear model.

y

x

The slope is 2.

The y-intercept is $\frac{1}{2}$.

POWER UP

You can write an equation for the linear model.

y

x

The slope is -1.

The y-intercept is 10.

The equation is $y = -x + 10$.

GO!

I see! I can identify the slope and y-intercept for linear models of real-world situations!

WORK TOGETHER

Samuel made a linear model of his data set to represent the total amount in his savings account since he started it. How much money did Samuel have in his savings account when he started it? How much did he save each week?

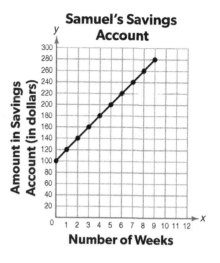

Samuel's Savings Account

Amount in Savings Account (in dollars)

Number of Weeks

- **Find the y-intercept.** When $x = 0$, $y = 100$.
  Samuel started with $100 in his savings account.

- **Find the slope.** The slope is 20. Samuel saved $20 each week.

A You can use the equation of a linear model to solve problems.

DO

The following equations represent the gallons of water, y, remaining in two different tanks x weeks after they started leaking. Which tank is leaking faster? Which tank started with more water?

Tank 1: $y = -3x + 10$

Tank 2: $y = -2x + 20$

I see! When $x = 0$, the tanks have been leaking for 0 weeks. So $(0, b)$, the y-intercept of each graph, represents the starting number of gallons of water in each tank.

1 Find and compare the slopes of the tanks.

2 Find the y-intercept for each tank.

The slope for Tank 1 is _____.

The slope for Tank 2 is _____.

Tank _____ is leaking faster.

The y-intercept for Tank 1 is _____.

The y-intercept for Tank 2 is _____.

Tank _____ started with more water.

DISCUSS Dena says she sees that $-3 < -2$. But she asks why, when comparing the slopes, -3 is considered to be leaking faster?

PRACTICE

Solve.

1 Sylvia made this linear model to represent the number of cups of dog food she will need for a given number of days. How many cups of dog food does her dog eat each day? _____

Cups of Dog Food Needed

2 Colleen made this linear model to represent the amount of fencing needed to enclose a square garden. As the side length of the square garden increases by 1 meter, how much more fencing will she need?

_____

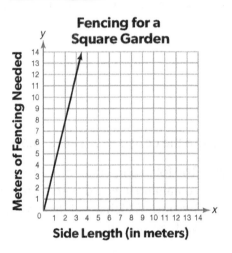

Fencing for a Square Garden

3 Jake made this linear model to represent the height of an airplane in feet x minutes after it begins its descent. What was the initial height of the airplane? _____

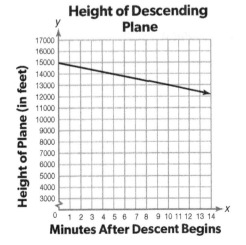

Height of Descending Plane

4 Steve made this linear model to represent the distance, y, in miles he's traveled after x hours. What was the rate of change of his distance? _____

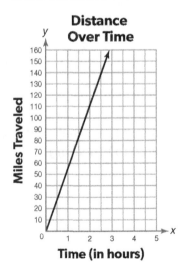

Distance Over Time

Solve.

5 Benny wrote the equation $y = 6x - 30$ to represent the depth of a diver under water as he swims to the surface. At what depth did the diver begin swimming to the surface?

_____

6 Olivia wrote the equation $y = 25x$ to represent the total amount of money she has saved after x months. How much money will Olivia save each month?

_____

Solve.

7 Julia wrote the equation $y = -2x + 100$ to represent the number of pencils remaining after x weeks. How many pencils did she start with? How many pencils does she use each week?

_____

8 Justin wrote the equation $y = \frac{1}{2}x + 3$ to represent the height of a plant after x days. What was the initial height, in centimeters, of the plant? How many centimeters does the plant grow each day?

_____

I remember! In a linear model in the form $y = mx + b$, m is the slope and b is the y-intercept.

 Model with Mathematics

Jill reads an order form for a company that makes shirts. She sees that the cost per shirt decreases as more shirts are ordered.

She writes the equation $y = -\frac{1}{2}x + 20$ to represent the cost per shirt when x shirts are ordered.

Based on her model, what is the rate of change in the cost for each

additional shirt ordered? _____

Jill says her model does not work because 40 shirts would cost $0 each.

Is Jill correct? _____

I see! A linear model may represent a data set well, but it may not make sense for values outside of the data set.

PROBLEM SOLVING

DATA STORAGE

READ

The graph shows the relationship between the total cost of online data storage and the number of gigabytes downloaded. Use the graph to determine the cost per gigabyte and the cost if 0 gigabytes are downloaded.

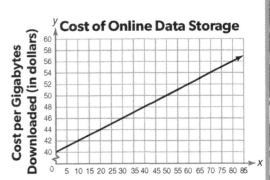

Cost of Online Data Storage

Cost per Gigabytes Downloaded (in dollars)

Number of Gigabytes Downloaded

PLAN

• Find the _____ per gigabyte downloaded (slope).

• Find the cost if _____ gigabytes are downloaded (y-intercept).

SOLVE

To find the slope, pick two points on the graph, such as (0, __40__) and (30, _____).

Calculate the slope using these points

$$\frac{\text{change in } y}{\text{change in } x} = \frac{\boxed{} - \boxed{}}{\boxed{} - \boxed{}} = \frac{\boxed{}}{\boxed{}} = \boxed{}$$

To find the y-intercept, find the point at which the graph intersects _____.

This point is (_____, _____), so the y-intercept is _____.

CHECK

Write the equation for the graph in slope-intercept form.

$y =$ _____ $x +$ _____

Substitute an x-value of a point on the line for x in the equation. Check that the y-value from the equation matches the y-value for that point on the graph.

Choose the point (50, _____).

$y =$ _____ $\times$ _____ $+$ _____

$y =$ _____ $+$ _____

$y =$ _____

Does the value you found for y match the y-value shown on the graph? _____

The cost per gigabyte downloaded is _____.

The cost if no gigabytes are downloaded is _____.

PRACTICE

Use the problem-solving steps to help you.

1 Nina gets paid $200 a week plus an extra $5 per handbag she sells. Write an equation for this problem, and identify the slope and y-intercept.

CHECKLIST
☐ READ
☐ PLAN
☐ SOLVE
☐ CHECK

2 Burt pays $20 a month for his water bill. The water company will add $0.01 per gallon used to his bill. Write an equation for this problem, and identify the slope and y-intercept.

CHECKLIST
☐ READ
☐ PLAN
☐ SOLVE
☐ CHECK

3 When Myla visits a fruit stand, she buys a bag of oranges for $2 and several pounds of grapes at $1.50 per pound. Write an equation for this problem, and identify the slope and y-intercept.

CHECKLIST
☐ READ
☐ PLAN
☐ SOLVE
☐ CHECK

Glossary

adjacent angles angles that share both a common side and a common vertex (Lesson 15)

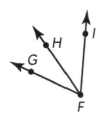

algebraic equation a number sentence with at least one variable that uses an equal sign to show equivalent quantities (Lesson 6)

$$x + 3 = 10$$
$$m - 1 = 3$$
$$4a = 12 + a$$
$$\frac{z}{3} = 6$$

algebraic expression a combination of numbers and/or variables joined by operations (Lesson 17)

$$x^2 - 5x + 3$$

alternate exterior angles angles that are outside two parallel lines and on opposite sides of the transversal (Lesson 15)

alternate interior angles angles that are between two parallel lines and on opposite sides of the transversal (Lesson 15)

arithmetic expression a combination of operations and numbers (Lesson 17)

$$6^2 - 5 \times 6 + 3$$

association the relationship between data points on a scatter plot (Lessons 18, 19)

base the repeated factor in a power (Lesson 2)

center of rotation the point around which a figure is rotated (Lesson 12)

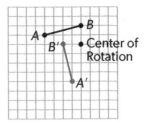

coefficient a number that is multiplied by a variable (Lesson 6)

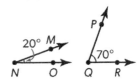

$$4x + 2 - 2x = 7x$$

coefficients

complementary angles angles whose measures sum to 90° (Lesson 15)

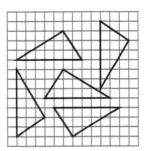

congruent having the same size and shape, but possibly different orientations (Lessons 10, 12)

corresponding angles the angles of two figures that are in the same relative position; angles that are in the same position when a transversal intersects two parallel lines (Lessons 10, 15)

corresponding sides the sides of two figures that are in the same relative position (Lesson 10)

cube number a number that is the product of the same three integer factors (Lesson 2)

cube root one of three equal factors of a number whose cube is equal to that number (Lesson 2)

cubic unit one three-dimensional cube used to measure volume (Lesson 17)

dilation a transformation that changes the size of a figure (Lesson 13)

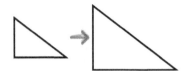

distributive property a property that states that the product of a factor and a sum is equal to the sum of the products of the factor and each addend; also applies to the product of a factor and a difference (Lesson 6)

$$4(a + 1) = (4 \cdot a) + (4 \cdot 1)$$
$$2(b - 3) = (2 \cdot b) - (2 \cdot 3)$$

exponent the raised number in a power that indicates the number of times the base is used as a factor (Lesson 2)

expression a mathematical phrase containing numbers and/or variables and operations (Lesson 6)

$$6 + 8$$
$$m - 1$$
$$5x + y$$
$$\frac{s}{2} + 3 - t$$

exterior angle an angle formed outside of a polygon by extending a side of the polygon (Lesson 15)

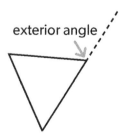

exterior angle

function a rule that assigns exactly one output value to each input value (Lesson 8)

x	1	2	3	4
y	2	0	−2	−4

hypotenuse the side opposite the right angle in a right triangle (Lesson 16)

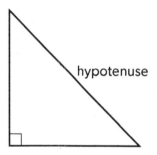

hypotenuse

image the figure that results from a transformation (Lessons 10, 12)

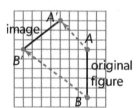

initial value an interpretation of the y-intercept of the graph of an equation in a real world situation (Lesson 8)

integers counting numbers (1, 2, 3, …), their opposites (−1, −2, −3, …), and zero (Lesson 6)

interior angle an angle inside a polygon that is formed by two sides of the polygon (Lesson 15)

interior angle

intersection the point or points where graphs of equations meet (Lesson 7)

irrational number a number whose decimal form does not repeat or terminate (Lesson 1)

legs the sides that form the right angle in a right triangle (Lesson 16)

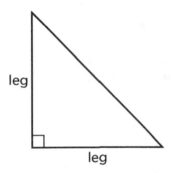

like terms terms that have the same variable raised to the same exponent (Lesson 6)

$$4x + 2 - 2x = 7x$$

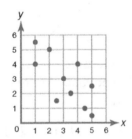

like terms

linear association a relationship shown on a scatter plot in which data points resemble a straight line (Lesson 18)

linear function a function whose graph is a straight line (Lesson 8)

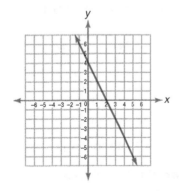

linear model a line that represents a data set and whose equation can be written in the form $y = mx + b$ (Lesson 20)

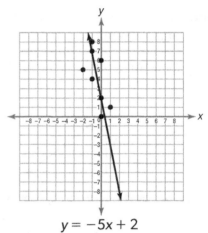

$$y = -5x + 2$$

This is a graph of a linear model.

line of reflection the line over which a figure is reflected (Lesson 11)

no association displaying no relationship of data points on a scatter plot (Lesson 18)

nonlinear association describes a scatter plot with points that resemble a curve (Lesson 18)

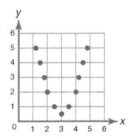

nonlinear function a function whose graph is not a straight line (Lesson 8)

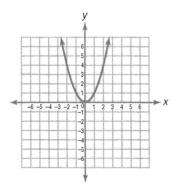

ordered pair the values of x and y that identify where a point is located on the x-y coordinate plane (Lesson 12)

order of operations rules for simplifying expressions with multiple operations
1) do what is inside parentheses first
2) evaluate exponents
3) multiply and divide from left to right
4) add and subtract from left to right (Lesson 17)

origin in the x-y coordinate plane, the point at which the x-axis and y-axis intersect; its coordinates are (0, 0) (Lesson 12)

outlier a data point whose value is very different from other data points on a scatter plot (Lessons 18 and 19)

power an expression of repeated multiplication (Lesson 2)

principal square root the nonnegative (positive) square root of a number (Lesson 2)

Pythagorean theorem In any right triangle, the sum of the squares of the lengths of the legs is equal to the square of the length of the hypotenuse. (Lesson 16)

quadrant one of the four sections of the x-y coordinate plane (Lesson 12)

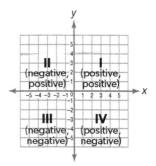

rate of change the ratio of the change in y-values to the corresponding change in x-values (Lesson 8)

rational number a number that can be written as the ratio of two integers (Lessons 1, 6)

$$4 = \frac{4}{1}$$
$$\frac{3}{4} = 0.75$$
$$-0.\overline{7} = -\frac{7}{9}$$

real number a rational number or an irrational number (Lesson 1)

reflection a flip of a figure over a line (Lesson 11)

repeating decimal a decimal that has a digit or a series of digits that repeat (Lesson 1)

$$0.\overline{1} = 0.1111111......$$
$$5.6\overline{43} = 5.64343434.....$$

rigid motion a transformation of a figure in a plane so that its size and shape remain unchanged (Lesson 10)

rotation a turn of a figure around a point (Lesson 12)

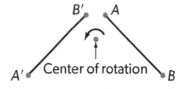

same-side interior angles angles that are between two parallel lines and on the same side of the transversal (Lesson 15)

scale numbers that change at regular intervals along an axis of a graph (Lesson 18)

scale drawing a drawing of a real object that has been enlarged or reduced by a scale factor (Lesson 13)

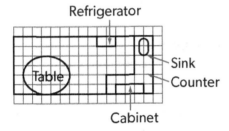

scale factor the ratio of the corresponding sides of a dilation (Lesson 13)

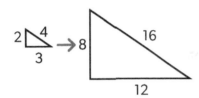

The scale factor is 4.

scatter plot a graph that shows ordered pairs of data as points (Lesson 18)

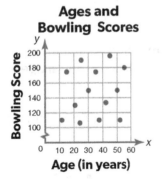

scientific notation a way to express numbers using a multiplication expression in which the first factor, the coefficient, is a number that is greater than or equal to 1 and less than 10, and the second factor is a power of 10 (Lesson 3)

similar having the same shape, but possibly having a different size (Lesson 14)

slope a ratio of the change in y-coordinates (*rise*) of a graph to the change in corresponding x-coordinates (*run*); the symbol for slope is m (Lessons 4, 5, 8, 20)

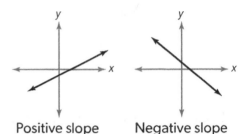

Positive slope   Negative slope

square number the product of an integer multiplied by itself (Lesson 2)

square root one of two equal factors of a number, each of whose square is equal to that number (Lessons 1, 2)

substitution the replacement of a variable with a numeric value (Lesson 17)

supplementary angles angles whose measures add up to 180° (Lesson 15)

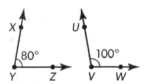

system of equations two or more equations with the same variables (Lesson 7)

Equation 1: $y = -2x + 4$

Equation 2: $y = x + 1$

terminating decimal a decimal that has a limited number of decimal places (Lesson 1)

$$8\frac{1}{25} = 8.04$$
$$= 8.040000000$$

translation a rigid motion in which a figure and its image have the same orientation (Lesson 10)

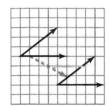

transversal a line that intersects two or more lines (Lesson 15)

trend line a straight line that best shows the linear relationship between data points on a scatter plot (Lesson 19)

unit rate a ratio that compares a quantity to 1 (Lesson 4)

variable a letter or symbol used to stand for one or more numbers (Lessons 6, 7)

$$4 + 7t = 25$$

The letter t is the variable. This algebraic equation is true when $t = 3$.

vertical angles opposite angles formed by two intersecting lines (Lesson 15)

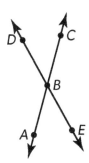

volume the amount of space taken up by a three-dimensional figure (Lesson 17)

x-axis the horizontal number line on an x-y coordinate graph (Lesson 18)

y-axis the vertical number line on an x-y coordinate graph (Lesson 18)

y-intercept the y-coordinate of the point at which a line crosses the y-axis (Lessons 5, 8, 20)

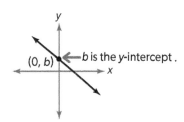

209

Name _____ Date _____

Math Tool: Dot Paper

Name _____ Date _____

Math Tool: Coordinate Grid

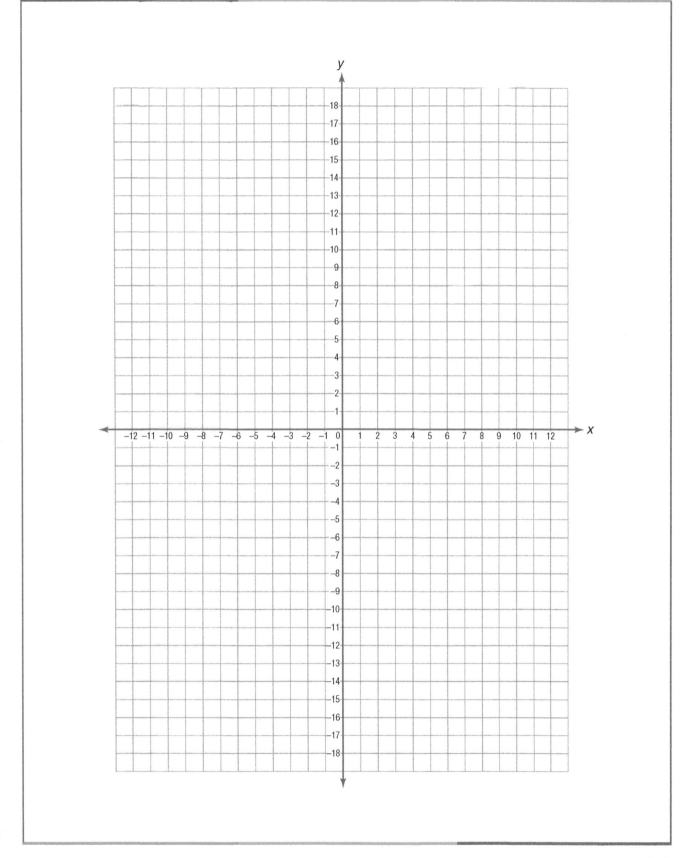

Math Tool: Coordinate Grid

Math Tool: **Properties of Multiplication**

Addition Properties
Associative Property of Addition $(a + b) + c = a + (b + c)$
Commutative Property of Addition $a + b = b + a$
Additive Identity Property of 0 $a + 0 = a$
Sum of Additive Inverses $a + (-a) = 0$

Multiplication Properties
Associative Property of Multiplication $(a \times b) \times c = a \times (b \times c)$
Commutative Property of Multiplication $a \times b = b \times a$
Multiplicative Identity Property of 1 $a \times 1 = a$
Product of Multiplicative Inverses $a \times \frac{1}{a} = 1$

Addition and Multiplication
Distributive Property of Multiplication over Addition $a \times (b + c) = (a \times b) + (a \times c)$
Distributive Property of Multiplication over Subtraction $a \times (b - c) = (a \times b) - (a \times c)$

Properties of Equality	
Addition Property of Equality If $a = b$, then $a + c = b + c$.	Multiplication Property of Equality If $a = b$, then $a \times c = b \times c$.
Subtraction Property of Equality If $a = b$, then $a - c = b - c$.	Division Property of Equality If $a = b$ and $c \neq 0$, then $a \div c = b \div c$.

Name _____ Date _____

Math Tool: Grid Paper

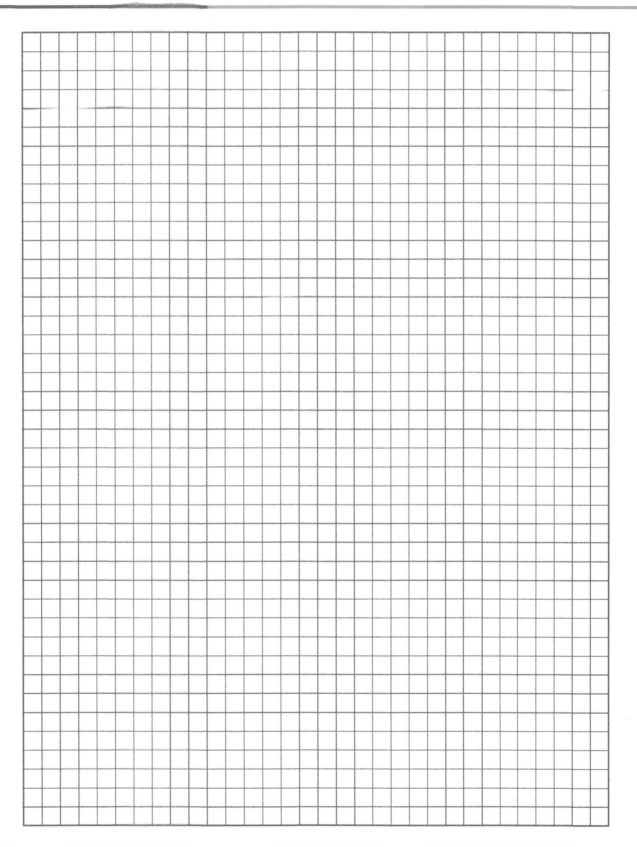

Name _____ Date _____

Math Tool: Grid Paper

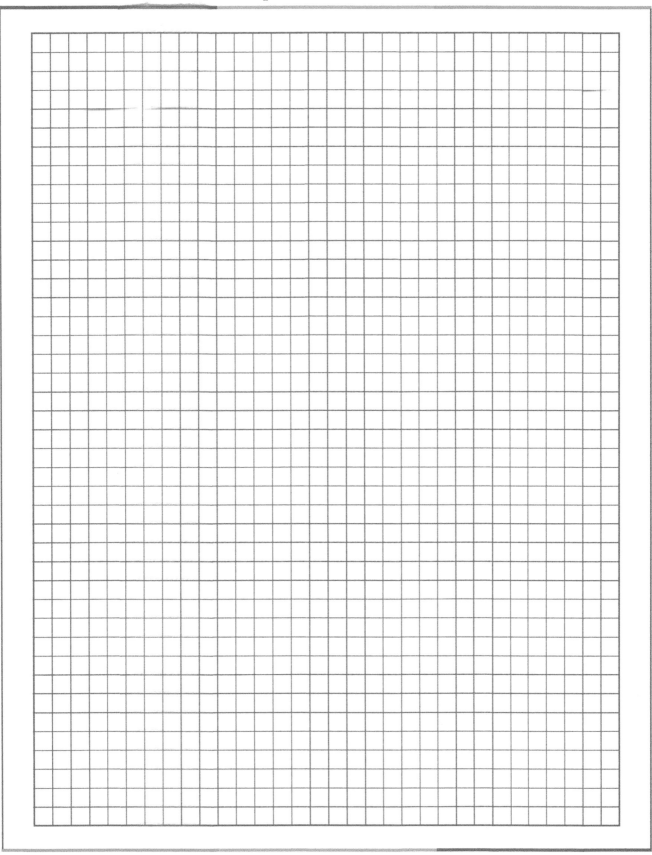

Math Tool: Pythagorean Theorem Proof

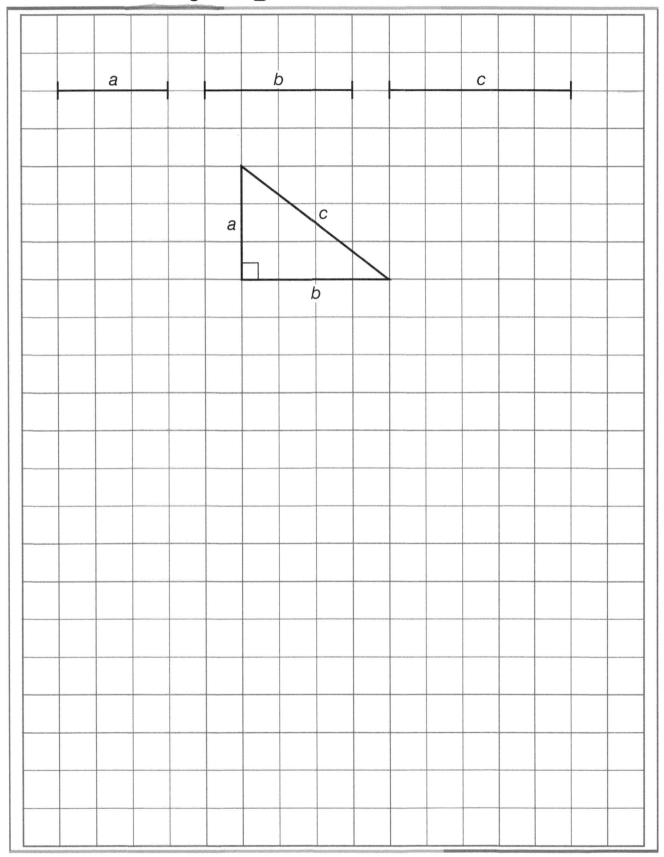

Name _____   Date _____

Math Tool: Volume Formulas

Formulas for Volume, *V*

Cylinder

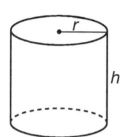

$$V = \pi r^2 h,$$

where *r* stands for the radius
and *h* stands for the height

Cone

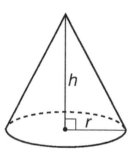

$$V = \frac{1}{3}\pi r^2 h,$$

where *r* stands for the radius
and *h* stands for the height

Sphere

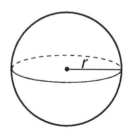

$$V = \frac{4}{3}\pi r^3,$$

where *r* stands for the radius

Pi, or π, is an irrational number than can be approximated as 3.14 or $\frac{22}{7}$.

Name _____ Date _____

Math Tool: Grid Paper

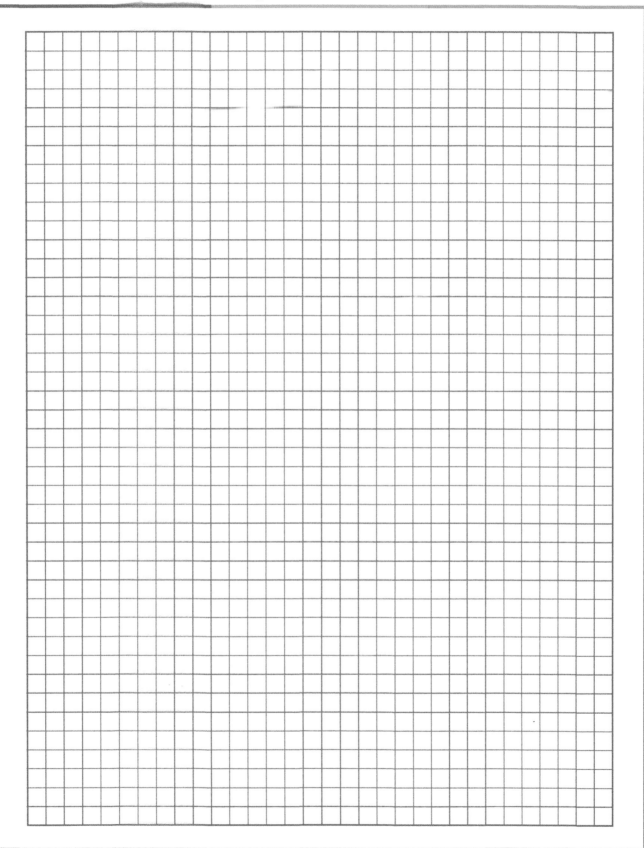

Name _____   Date _____

Math Tool: Volume Formulas

Formulas for Volume, *V*

Rectangular Prism

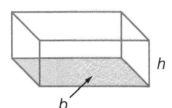

$V = b \times h,$

where *V* stands for the volume,
b stands for the area of the base,
and *h* stands for the height.

Rectangular Prism

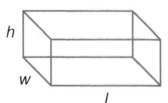

$V = l \times w \times h,$

where *V* stands for the volume,
l stands for the length,
w stands for the width,
and *h* stands for the height.

Name _____   Date _____

Math Tool: Grid Paper

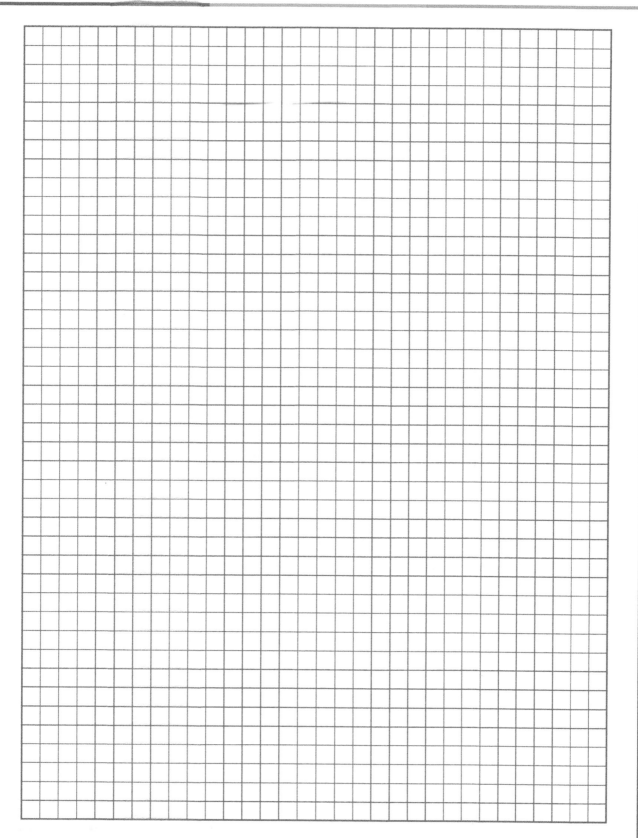

Name _____   Date _____

Math Tool: Coordinate Grids

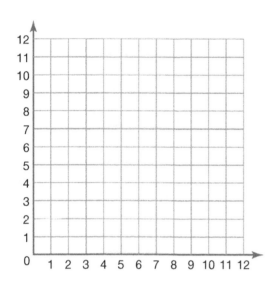

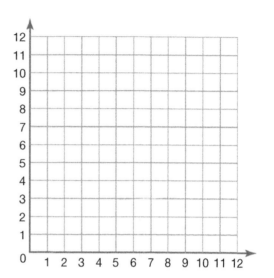

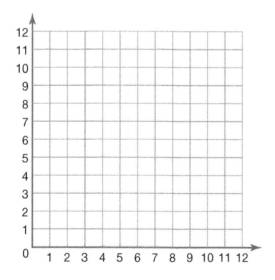

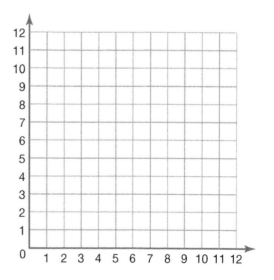

Name _____   Date _____

Math Tool: Coordinate Grids

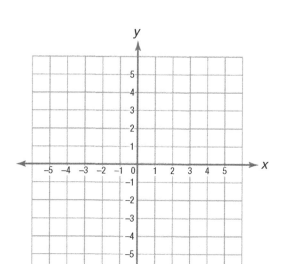

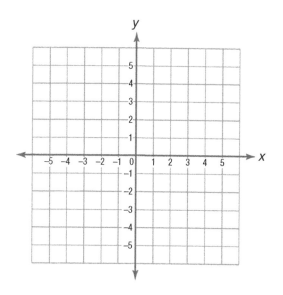

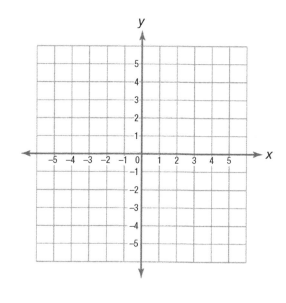

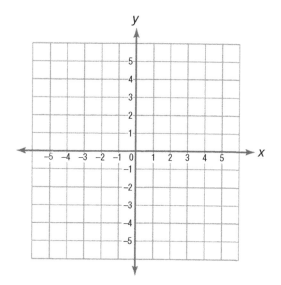

Math Tool: Fraction Strips

1

$\frac{1}{2}$	$\frac{1}{2}$

$\frac{1}{3}$	$\frac{1}{3}$	$\frac{1}{3}$

$\frac{1}{4}$	$\frac{1}{4}$	$\frac{1}{4}$	$\frac{1}{4}$

$\frac{1}{5}$	$\frac{1}{5}$	$\frac{1}{5}$	$\frac{1}{5}$	$\frac{1}{5}$

$\frac{1}{6}$	$\frac{1}{6}$	$\frac{1}{6}$	$\frac{1}{6}$	$\frac{1}{6}$	$\frac{1}{6}$

$\frac{1}{8}$	$\frac{1}{8}$	$\frac{1}{8}$	$\frac{1}{8}$	$\frac{1}{8}$	$\frac{1}{8}$	$\frac{1}{8}$	$\frac{1}{8}$

$\frac{1}{10}$	$\frac{1}{10}$	$\frac{1}{10}$	$\frac{1}{10}$	$\frac{1}{10}$	$\frac{1}{10}$	$\frac{1}{10}$	$\frac{1}{10}$	$\frac{1}{10}$	$\frac{1}{10}$

$\frac{1}{12}$	$\frac{1}{12}$	$\frac{1}{12}$	$\frac{1}{12}$	$\frac{1}{12}$	$\frac{1}{12}$	$\frac{1}{12}$	$\frac{1}{12}$	$\frac{1}{12}$	$\frac{1}{12}$	$\frac{1}{12}$	$\frac{1}{12}$

Name _____ Date _____

Math Tool: Coordinate Grid

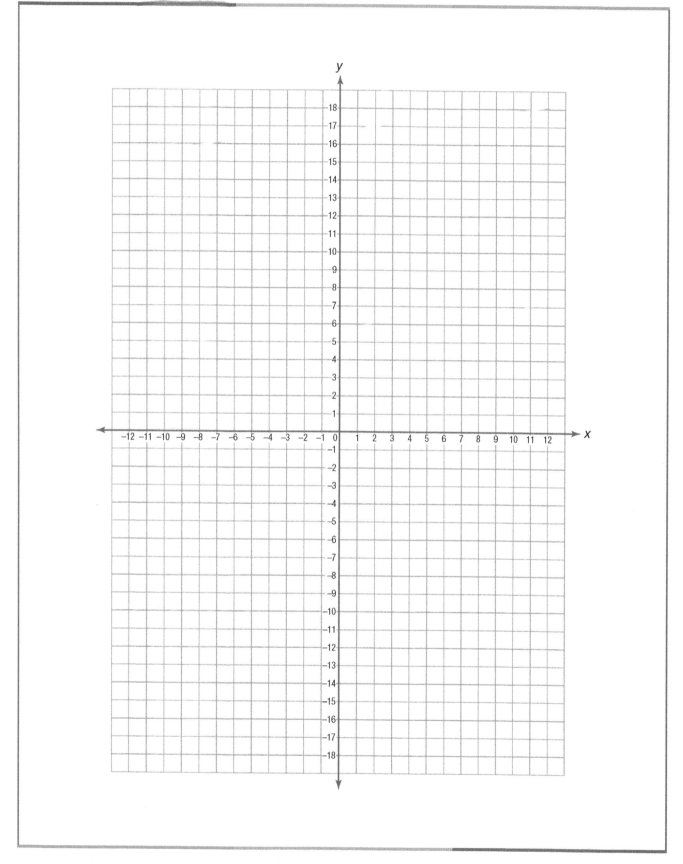

Math Tool: Coordinate Grid

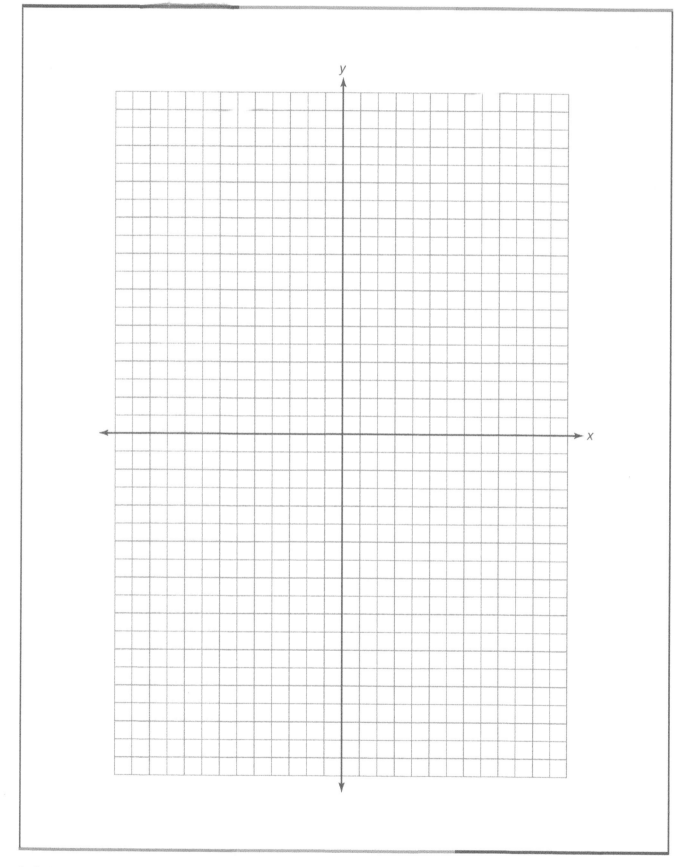

Name _____ Date _____

Math Tool: Grids

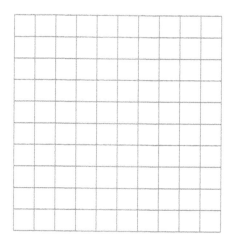

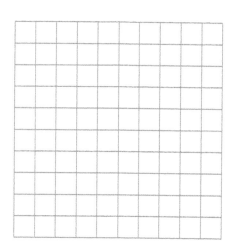

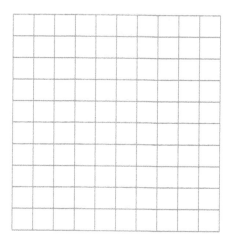

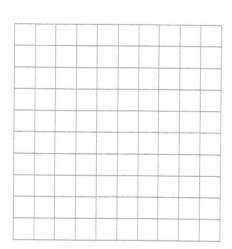

Name _____ Date _____

Math Tool: Two-Dimensional Shapes

circle
0 sides
0 angles

oval
0 sides
0 angles

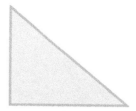

triangle
3 sides
3 angles

square
4 equal sides
4 right angles

rectangle
4 sides
4 right angles

rhombus
4 equal sides
4 angles

pentagon
5 sides
5 angles

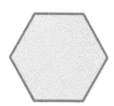

hexagon
6 sides
6 angles

octagon
8 sides
8 angles

octagon
8 sides
8 angles

hexagon
6 sides
6 angles

pentagon
5 sides
5 angles

Notes

Notes

Notes

Notes

Notes

Notes

Notes

Notes

Notes

Notes

Notes

Notes

Common Core Support Coach

TARGET ▶ Foundational Mathematics

Developed Exclusively for the CCSS

Master the key concepts you need to succeed in math!

FOCUS ON

- > Irrational Numbers
- > Square and Cube Roots
- > Scientific Notation
- > Proportionality and Slope
- > Equations and Functions
- > Transformations
- > Similarity and Triangles
- > The Pythagorean Theorem
- > Volume
- > Scatter Plots

www.triumphlearning.com

Phone: (800) 338-6519 • Fax: (866) 805-5723 • E-mail: customerservice@triumphlearning.com

ISBN-13: 978-1-61997-979-6

90000

9 781619 979796

T203NA

triumphlearning™

Coach® | Coach Digital™ | Buckle Down®